Palgrave Studies in Institutions, Economics and Law

Series Editors
Alain Marciano, University of Montpellier, Montpellier, France
Giovanni Ramello, University of Eastern Piedmont, Alessandria, Italy

Law and Economics is an interdisciplinary field of research that has emerged in recent decades, with research output increasing dramatically and academic programmes in law and economics multiplying. Increasingly, legal cases have an economic dimension and economic matters depend on rules and regulations. Increasingly, economists have realized that "institutions matter" because they influence economic activities. Increasingly, too, economics is used to improve our understanding of how institutions and how legal systems work. This new Palgrave Pivot series studies the intersection between law and economics, and addresses the need for greater interaction between the two disciplines.

More information about this series at
https://link.springer.com/bookseries/15241

Antonio Manganelli · Antonio Nicita

Regulating Digital Markets

The European Approach

Antonio Manganelli
University of Rome LUMSA
Rome, Italy

Antonio Nicita
University of Rome LUMSA
Rome, Italy

ISSN 2662-6535   ISSN 2662-6543 (electronic)
Palgrave Studies in Institutions, Economics and Law
ISBN 978-3-030-89387-3   ISBN 978-3-030-89388-0 (eBook)
https://doi.org/10.1007/978-3-030-89388-0

This Palgrave Macmillan imprint is published by the registered company Springer Nature Switzerland AG
The registered company address is: Gewerbestrasse 11, 6330 Cham, Switzerland

To Bernardo, Cosimo, Davide e Simone,
because tomorrow's world belongs to our children.,
but our thoughts and decisions today start shaping it.

PREFACE

Digital markets constitute a multifold and multi-layered ecosystem, whose core backbone is made of very high capacity fixed and mobile telecom infrastructures. Those physical infrastructures play a fundamental role by interconnecting users and allowing data communication. Nevertheless, they probably are neither the brain nor the soul of the digital ecosystem. Services, contents, applications, and their providers permeate and shape the digital markets and digital society with sophisticated, pervasive, self-nurturing networks made of economic and social interactions, taking place at various levels in the materiality-immateriality scale.

Digital markets are not a sector of the economy. In fact, there is no such a thing as a digital sector. Digital transformation and digital markets extend horizontally across the entire economy and across all sectors, as well as across the whole society. They also naturally extend geographically, across countries and globally, beyond all political borders.

It goes without saying that the architecture and the functioning of such a system are extremely complex and dynamic, due to its incredibly dense and extended web of interactions and interdependences, on one side, and its exponential (r)evolutionary pace, on the other side. Stakeholders approaching digital markets, e.g., consumers, business users, researchers, policy makers, or regulators, are therefore constantly subject to the risk of analysing specific aspects of the system in an isolated way, or taking decisions subject to inertia or path dependency. In the former case, they would risk to neglect some important aspects or dynamics within the system, possibly producing unintended consequences, while, in the latter, they would risk adopting ineffective, inefficient, or detrimental choices based on outdated information or conditions.

It is indeed quite difficult to get a sound understanding of digital markets functioning and its effect on economy and society; therefore it has been equally arduous for public bodies to govern its dynamics and develop an effective and fair digital policy. This book focuses precisely on the challenges that regulators and policy makers have faced and will face in the transition from the 'old' (network) industries to the new digital ecosystem. Our intent is to describe, in one succinct book, the evolution of the digital economy, its main actors, notably the global digital platforms, as well as its interactions, interdependences, and trade-offs, eventually proposing insights about why public rules are needed, what kind of rules could be more effective, fair, and efficient, and who should pose and enforce them.

Indeed, the digital ecosystem is full of economic and legal interdependences, entanglements, trade-offs, and (apparent) paradoxes. Just to mention a few examples among the several debated within the book, the Digital Market Society is a place where: (i) digital markets, inherently borderless, used to have grater cross-border obstacles than 'bricks-and-mortar' markets; (ii) unregulated platforms create their own (algorithmic) private rules, aiming to extend their effect toward all (*erga omnes*); (iii) information and communication flows are almost limitless but tend to become artificially 'chambered'; (iv) big digital companies aim to become markets; (v) digital economy have many different faces and digital markets have many different sides; (vi) platforms know so well our preferences to anticipate our needs and even our order requests; (vii) an increase of consumers satisfaction (in terms of preference-matching) may come along with a reduction of consumer surplus; (viii) "free" services are not free at all, yet implicitly exchanged against economicly valuable personal data; (ix) search costs are extremely low as well as users' interest to seek information; (x) the digital information system's most valuable service is not to describe facts but to create emotions.

We do not even try to provide any definitive answer or solution to those digital trade-offs. Our aim is to provide a small contribution to the

wider academic and policy debate, which has been roaming and fluctu-
ating, yet is progressively building a "Digital Compass"[1] tracing a 'Path to
the Digital Decade' and more generally towards the targets and governance for the digital world of tomorrow, in Europe and in the rest of
the world.[2]

This book is composed of an introduction and two parts. The Introduction deals with *Digital Transformation, Big Techs, and Public Policies*:
it provides a general conceptual and thematic framework to the following
analysis but could also be read as a stand-alone paper. The following chapters expand on the specific arguments raised in the introduction and are
grouped in two parts: (I) *The Evolution of Digital Markets and Digital
Rights*, and (II) *Regulating Big Tech's Impact on Market and Society*. In
addition, thematic boxes are included throughout the book to elucidate
and better analyse some specific issues.

Just as the digital ecosystem is grounded on telecom infrastructures
and services, this work builds on a previous recent book of ours, exploring
The Governance of the Telecom Markets. From the telecom perspective,
digital platforms provide services "over the top" (OTT) of the traditional
telecom value-chain. Similarly, this new book should be read (and stored
on bookshelves) "on the top" of the previous one. For many aspects,
repeatedly represented in both books, telecom, media, and digital markets
and services are strictly interrelated—either as complements or substitutes—and therefore they should be jointly analysed, and their regulations
and policies should be jointly conceived and implemented.

The meaning of the book's secondary title is twofold. This book
outlines *the European approach* to digital market regulation, in the
sense that we mainly examine EU law, yet also US rules and policies are considered. Notwithstanding, considering the scope and nature
of digital markets and players, most of the economic and institutional
issues addressed are inherently global phenomena, common to all countries, economies, and societies. In addition, *the European approach* also
underlines that European policy makers, as far as digital markets are
concerned, are still approaching a systemic policy design, which has not
been completely achieved yet. Although the EU has developed digital

---

[1] EU Commission (2021) Digital Compass 2030—The European way for the Digital
Decade.

[2] EU Commission (2021) Proposal for a Decision establishing the 2030
Policy Programme "Path to the Digital Decade".

policies for more than a decade, only recently a comprehensive and clear design is emerging: fundamental cornerstones will be laid with the final approval of the Digital Service Act and the Digital Market Act (the Commission proposals are described and analysed in the book).

The digital revolution has indeed re-shaped traditional approaches concerning production, consumption, and distributions. It has transformed economic, social, and political interactions, in all countries, all industries, and is progressively embracing all aspects of life. This is an epochal transformation, fascinating and exciting, source of countless new opportunities, yet, at the same time, source of great concerns.

Here comes our composite motivation for this book. As scholars, we strongly feel the intellectual need to devote our time to study and investigate these alluring and momentous phenomena; as fathers, we strive to leave to our children a future-proof world, able to exploit the growth opportunities brought by digital transformation yet trying to control and minimise its risks; finally, as civil servants, we constantly feel the ethical need to give our day-to-day contribution to develop and implement sound public policies. Indeed, we do believe that, also within digital markets, public intervention does matters: it is public authorities' responsibility to determine a fair and efficient alignment between private interests, public interest, and social welfare.

Rome, Italy   Antonio Manganelli
                                                       Antonio Nicita

ACKNOWLEDGEMENTS

Our work is based on our academic research as well as on our professional experience as civil servants in regulatory and competition authorities across Europe. This very book about Digital markets (D), as well as the previous one about the Governance of Telecom markets (T), are the result of our common vision, however the two introductory sections (T.1, D.1) have been jointly drafted, whereas AM has drafted sections T.2, T.3, T.4, T.6, T.8, D.2, D.3, D.4, D.6 and AN sections T.5, T.7, D.5, D.7. For many fruitful discussions around all these topics, held over the years, we would like to **thank**: Giuseppe Abbamonte, Giuliano Amato, Laura Ammannati, Diego Agus, Marco Bani, Marco Botta, Eric Brousseau, Chiara Caccinelli, Cristina Caffarra, Carlo Cambini, Maja Cappello, Chiara Carrozza, Sabino Cassese, Martin Cave, Filomena Chirico, Andrea Coscelli, Stefano da Empoli, Isabella De Michelis, Alexandre De Streel, Antonio De Tommaso, Fabiana di Porto, Filippo Donati, Veronica Gaffey, Davide Gallino, Elisa Giomi, Giorgio Greppi, Celine Kauffmann, Carmen Lembo, Benedetta Liberatore, Paolo Lupi, Michela Manetti, Stefano Mannoni, Alain Marciano, Lucia Marzialetti, Sandro Mendonça, Giorgio Monti, Giulio Napolitano, Jorge Padilla, Pier Luigi Parcu, Antonio Perrucci, Nicolas Petit, Andrea Pezzoli, Anna Pisarkiewicz, Giovanni Pitruzzella, Oreste Pollicino, Augusto Preta, Giovanni Ramello, Nicoletta Rangone, Andrea Renda, Maria Alessandra Rossi, Lorenzo Saltari, Marco Scialdone, Guido

Scorza, Alessandro Sindici, Guido Stazi, Alessandra Tonazzi, Tommaso Valletti, Roberto Viola, Paolo Visca, and Anthony Whelan.

Special thanks are due: Oscar Borgogno, Giuseppe Colangelo, Marco Delmastro, Valeria Falce, Maria Luce Mariniello, Emanuela Michetti, Paola Guarino, and Lorenzo Principali.

CONTENTS

ABOUT THE AUTHORS

Antonio Manganelli, Ph.D. is professor of Antitrust & Regulation at LUMSA University (Italy) and adjunct professor of Competition Law and Policy at the University of Siena (Italy). Since March 2021, he has worked as Deputy Head of Cabinet for the Italian Ministry of Economic Development, coordinating telecom, media, and digital markets policymaking. He previously served in other public institutions, i.e., the Italian Regulatory Authority for Telecom, Media, and Postal sectors (AGCOM), the UK Competition and Markets Authority (CMA), the Office of the Body of European Regulators for Electronic Communications (BEREC), the research department at the Italian Central Bank (Banca d'Italia). Antonio Manganelli was also research associate at the European University Institute (EUI). He holds a M.Sc. in Political Science and Economic Policy and a Ph.D. in Law and Economics from the University of Siena.

Antonio Nicita, Ph.D. is full professor of Economic Policy at LUMSA University (Italy). He is also member of the Regulatory Scrutiny Board at the European Commission. He previously served as Commissioner of the Italian Regulatory Authority for Telecom, Media, and Postal sectors (AGCOM) and as member of the Steering Group in Regulation & Emerging Technologies at the Organisation for Economic Development and Cooperation (OECD). Before starting his academic carrier, Antonio Nicita also worked as an economist at the Italian Competition Authority (AGCM) and as advisor to regulatory and competition matters for the International Competition Network (ICN). Antonio Nicita was Visiting Fulbright Professor at Yale University (USA), Visiting Scholar at the University of Paris X-Nanterre (France) and at the European University Institute (EU), and Visiting Researcher at the University of Cambridge (UK). He holds an M.Sc. in Economic and Social Sciences from the Bocconi University in Milan, and a Ph.D. in Economics from the University of Siena.

List of Figures

LIST OF TABLES

LIST OF BOXES

CHAPTER 1

INTRODUCTION: Digital Transformation, Big Techs, and Public Policies

Abstract Digital transformation has profoundly affected economic, social, and political spheres for years, progressively creating a Digital Market Society. Today's main actors are a few global platforms (so called 'Big Techs'), which are at the core of a complex and multifaceted digital ecosystem cutting across all industries, markets, and societies. Their relevance in terms of economic and informational power is unprecedented, yet public bodies have struggled to deeply understand how to effectively discipline their activity and their impact on market dynamics and information pluralism. Recently, some important public actions have been taken, or planned, on both side of the Atlantic, in order to regulate Big Techs' impact on economy and society.

Keywords Digital Transformation · Big Techs · Market power · Pluralism · Public policy

1.1 The Evolution of the Digital Market Society

The locution 'Digital transformation' indicates a set of technological, cultural, organizational, social, creative and managerial changes associated

© The Author(s), under exclusive license to Springer Nature Switzerland AG 2022
A. Manganelli and A. Nicita, *Regulating Digital Markets*,
Palgrave Studies in Institutions, Economics and Law,
https://doi.org/10.1007/978-3-030-89388-0_1

with digital technology applications in all aspects of human society. [1] *Erik Stolterman e Anna Croon Fors, Information Technology and the Good Life, in Information Systems Research: Relevant Theory and Informed Practice, 2004, p. 689, ISBN 1-4020-8094-8.* By acting in a systemic and combined way on these elements the digital transformation goes beyond the simple adoption of new technologies and allows, on one side, to provide services, goods and experiences, and on the other side, to find, to process and to make accessible large quantities of contents, creating pervasive new connections between people, places and things. [2] *Mark P. McDonald, Andy Rowsell-Jones - The Digital Edge, Exploiting Information and Technology for Business Advantage -Gartner, Inc., 2012.*[1]

The digital transformation of economy and society is based on rapid and often disruptive innovations involving more and more individuals, businesses, and objects, having a global rather than national dimension. Indeed, digital transformation involves all sectors and all countries, and its global relevance is confirmed by the United Nations Sustainable Development Goals, which set access to information and communications technology and universal and affordable access to the Internet as keys to a future sustainable world.[2]

The "great digital transformation", paraphrasing Karl Polanyi's conceptualisation of the English industrial revolution and bringing it to XXI century,[3] is thus shaping a completely new "market society", a digital one, where new norms of consumption, modes of production, institutions, business models, and individual interactions emerge. In the "digital market society" all previous social, economic, and political dimensions of life have dramatically changed. Indeed, many thinkers claim that today we are just at the beginning of a new co-evolutionary path leading towards an epochal revolution.

---

[1] This definition was extracted on 23 January 2020 from the Wikipedia page "digital transformation", selecting the Italian language: https://it.wikipedia.org/wiki/Digital_t ransformation (according to our opinion, the English one was not satisfactory). The content of the page was then translated in English via Google Translate, which has been "humanly" proof-read after having bought the reference books on Amazon (one book and one kindle version). On 1 May 2020, a sentence from this same quotation was posted on Antonio Manganelli's facebook page and twitted by Antonio Nicita's Twitter profile. The bizarre description of this process is itself part of the definition of digital transformation.

[2] UN Resolution (2015).

[3] Polany (1944).

Like each long journey, the digital transformation has begun with a single step, and proceeded step by step: at the beginning there were telecommunications networks, then the internet came and afterword the Web and its evolutions.

Box 1.1 Internet and Web

Internet and Web are very often used interchangeably as synonymous, whereas they are two different concepts, yet strictly interrelated. The Internet is a network of interconnected networks. Those networks, and indirectly all devices hosted, communicate via the Internet protocol suite (TCP/IP), carrying information and services such as electronic emails, voice over IP and also the Word Wide Web ("the Web"). So, the Internet is a network, or better the Net(work), and the Web is a service carried by the Net.

Indeed, the Web, created by English scientist Tim Berners-Lee Web in 1989, is an information system service running over the internet, where information resources are identified by a Uniform Resource Locator (URL or web address), which is made accessible to users by a software application, i.e., a web browser, communicating via the Hypertext Transfer Protocol (HTTP), with another software application, i.e., a web server, responsible for processing the information requests.

As for the deployment of telecom networks, both competitive dynamics within the markets (unlocked by liberalisation and pro-competitive regulation) and public industrial policy incentivised and pushed for innovative investments: in 2020, very high-capacity networks (VHCNs) cover almost 60% of EU households, and 33% of the households have an Ultrafast BB connection (Fig. 1.1).

Indeed, the EU has progressively designed public industrial policies for VHCNs investments, by setting increasingly ambitious connectivity and broadband targets: from the challenging yet achievable goals established within the 2010 Digital Agenda for Europe (DAE)[4] to the extremely

---

[4] European Commission (2010).

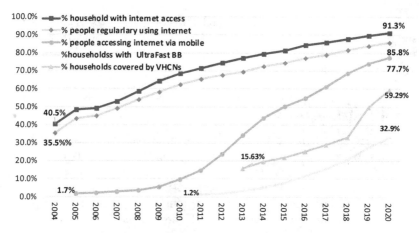

Fig. 1.1 Fixed and Mobile Internet development in EU (*Source* EU Commission – Digital Scoreboard 2020)

ambitious objectives within the 2016 Gigabit Society (GS).[5] In a nutshell, the DAE asked Member States and undertakings to reach, by 2020, a universal availability of at least 30 Mbps for all EU households and 100 Mbps for 50% of EU households. The GS overall goal is to ensure, by 2025, a Gigabit connectivity (i.e., 1 Gbps = 1000 Mbps) for all main socio-economic drivers (e.g., education buildings, government services, transport hubs, digitally intensive enterprises) and a universal access to at least 100 Mbps, extendable to 1 Gbps, for all European households, even in rural and remote areas. The 2021 Digital Compass (DC)[6] finally prescribes that extension to be completed by 2030, thus providing 1 Gigabit for everyone.

The digital transformation has been indeed driven by the transformation of telecom networks and services, namely: (a) digitisation, progressively involving all information and signals, (b) development of new transmission techniques on the Internet protocol, and (c) the enhancement of internet networks' transmission capacity, allowing larger and larger mass of data and contents to be delivered. It became therefore

[5] European Commission (2016b).

[6] EU Commission (2021) Digital Compass 2030—The European way for the Digital Decade.

possible delivering written messages, voice traffic, editorial contents and videos through the same transmission platform, enabling their reception with the same device.

As a consequence, the number of internet connections has constantly grown, increasing the amount of users interconnected and regularly using internet. Moreover, the development of mobile internet increased exponentially the ability and willingness of users to stay connected "anytime, anywhere".[7]

As far as the web's evolution is concerned, during all the nineties, the Web was mainly composed of static websites, allowing no or minimal users' interactions, such as standard hypertext navigation between web pages and the use of web search engines. In the new millennium, in the so-called *web 2.0* era, the web started to increase its participative features—enabled by the increasing quality (performance and security) of connectivity, thus allowing and facilitating users' interactions and collaboration. Users started to actively create contents and not just passively consuming them, finally establishing virtual social communities as building blocks of a digital market society.

The same digital transformation, that pushed towards the web 2.0 and beyond, also transformed businesses and widened economic interactions via internet (see Sect. 2). From the mere trading in online shops, which needed many additional off-line actions, the internet economy has been shaped into several diverse forms of digital capitalism.[8] Some examples are the *sharing and collaborative economy*, immersive e-commerce and marketplaces, often implemented by digital multi-sided platforms, acting as "matchmakers" among different groups of consumers and/or businesses.[9] Moreover, within the digital market society, especially with the increasing use of mobile internet, all interactions, transactions, consumption and production became an unlimited source of data, which became an economic key asset and productive factor.

The most recent step concerning the digital transformation of our society and economy is the Internet of Things (IoT), a network of objects ("things") interconnected and connected to internet, which communicate

[7] Manganelli and Nicita (2020).

[8] Schiller (2000).

[9] Evans and Schmalensee (2016).

and exchange information with limited human interaction. These innovations have transformed consumers' markets, and also set the base for what is called the fourth industrial revolution, a.k.a., the "industry 4.0". The First Industrial Revolution used water and steam power to mechanise production. The Second one used electric power to create mass production. The Third one, started in the second half of the last century, used electronics and information technology to automate production. Now, a Fourth Industrial Revolution is building on the Third one. Indeed, there are distinctive reasons why today's digital transformations represent an additional revolutionary step different from the previous one: (a) velocity, having an exponential rather than linear development; (b) connectivity, based on very high capacity fixed and mobile networks and the IoT; and (c) immateriality, supported by innovative web applications, artificial intelligence, cloud computing, and big data.[10]

Within this context, creating a European Digital Single Market (DSM) has been considered a far-reaching priority to boost EU digital economy and society. However, fragmentation of rules at national level, as well as a widespread lack of consumers' trust on online transactions, notably for cross-country ones, represented relevant impediments, which EU policy makers had to progressively tackle (Sect. 3).

The *digital market society* is nowadays a networked multi-layered ecosystem, whose fundamental backbone is composed of very high capacity fixed and mobile communications physical infrastructures, which probably are neither its brain nor its soul. Services, contents, applications, and their providers permeate the digital society with sophisticated, pervasive, self-nurturing networks made of economic, social, and operational interactions (human and non-human), taking place at various levels of the materiality-immateriality scale.

This ecosystem is extremely complex, and it is populated by a wide range of diverse actors:

- organizations, running very different kind of business or providing public services, e.g., ICT manufacturers, network operators, communications service providers, a multitude of digital platforms, creative content producers, advertisers, applications producers, 'vertical

---

[10] Schwab (2016).

companies', i.e., industries horizontally impacted by digital transformation (for example, automotive, energy, food and agriculture, healthcare, manufacturing, transportation and logistics and so on);
- mid and end-users consuming different kind of digital and ICT products, e.g., private and public organisations, "digital champions",[11] digital experts and unsophisticated consumers.

Within the digital ecosystem, digital platforms are crucial actors. From the perspective of telecom industry, they are often called Over-The-Top providers (OTTs), as they provide services to users via the public internet and telecoms infrastructures, but "over the top" of the traditional telecom markets' value-chain. As a matter of fact, within the digital transformation, the linear value chain of the industrial economy has been replaced with a non-linear (modular) platforms' ecosystems. The digital market society comprises a multitude of OTTs, having a broad scope of activities: for example, online advertising, marketplace services, internet search engines, social media, creative contents aggregations and distribution, video-sharing, communications services, products price comparison, application distribution, payment system services, collaborative activities, etc.[12]

'New economies' brought a great deal of innovation and economic value; nonetheless platform and data economies started to raise concerns about fundamental individual rights. Indeed, there are crucial economic entanglements and trade-offs between, on one side, the static and dynamic market value of digital economy and, on the other side, privacy, consumers' rights, access rights, and even free speech and pluralism.

Despite those crucial aspects, the development of public policies for digital markets was not an easy process, and it is still nowadays quite convoluted and unsettled. This is mainly due the continuous and fast innovation, making public bodies often lagging behind in terms of understanding of new technologies and their impact on markets and society. Moreover, digital markets have been subject to an intended

---

[11] Establishing a group of EU "Digital Champions" is one of the policy within the Digital Single Market strategy put in place by the European Union: each EU member state appoints a Digital Champion to support the establishment of an inclusive digital society and to advise the European Commission. https://ec.europa.eu/digital-single-market/en/digital-champions.

[12] Van DijcK, Poell and De Waal (2018); EU Commission (2016a); BEREC (2016).

cautious (i.e., light-touch) regulatory approach, in order to minimise the risk that an imbalanced intervention could hinder innovation. Regulatory solutions, such as "wait and see", "business as usual" or "overseen self-regulation",[13] did not represent effective policies and regulatory instruments, and indeed did not build an effective governance for new digital markets and the new social interactions intermediated by digital platforms.

In this framework, "platforms enact the rules that their users must follow when they interact; as such they have a role as 'private rule makers' or 'private regulators,' which organize the exchange between large number of users. These private rules affect the efficiency of economic exchange but also the benefits of participation in the platform."[14] Therefore platforms developed somehow a private legal ordering (or few ones, dividing the cyberspace, as in a partition), where rule-making and enforcement was somehow based on their economic and bargaining power. Those private orderings were (a) not subject (or not effectively subject) to public rules, because of public bodies' limited regulatory capacity in the digital world;[15] and did (b) not need to rely on "traditional" public law-enforcement mechanisms, also with concern of the material exclusion of a single user from the community, as platforms have the capacity (i.e., the material power) to exclude individuals from their community: in the cyberspace, virtual coercion is indeed materially effective (Sect. 4.1).

A public regulatory intervention has therefore become crucial for a fair and effective functioning of the Digital Market Society, bringing back to public authorities the leading role of rulemaking for those fundamental digital rights, e.g., consumer protection in e-commerce and online services; universal and non-discriminatory access to web and its contents;

---

[13] This is the case, for example, regarding the commitments that Facebook, Google, Mozilla, Microsoft and Twitter have signed, joining in 2018 the European Code of Practice of self-regulation on online disinformation.

[14] Crawford, Crémer, Dinielli, Fletcher, Heidhues, Schnitzer, Scott Morton, and Seim (2021).

[15] The concept of regulatory capacity is based onto the formal and substantive ability of public bodies to impose effective obligations, creating an efficient and socially desirable outcome in markets and society. For some application see BEREC (2013) Report on the NRAs' regulatory capacity; OECD (2009) about Better Regulation in Europe.

online privacy and data protection; cyber security and internet security (Sect. 4), as well as contrast to illegal and harmful online contents (Sect. 7).

Some sectoral regulators and policy makers recently opened dialogues and made attempts to co-regulate those ecosystems[16] or anyway tried to steer "platforms law". Notwithstanding, many authorities have been complaining about the lack of inspection and audit powers on the platforms, their operating algorithms, their data collection, aggregation and use-flows, which ultimately would allow to verify the impact of private (or public–private) rules that global platforms have given themselves.

A clear, comprehensive, and advanced regulatory policy has been designed and put in place in Europe with regards to data protection (GDPR) and consumer protection. Yet, there were widespread doubts about the effectiveness of such an approach limiting ex-ante regulation to protection of personal rights, even if complemented by competition law enforcement.

1.2 BIG TECHS' BURST: THE RISE OF DIGITAL POWERS AND ANTITRUST REACTIONS

Digital platforms play a crucial role in today's economy, have a broad scope of different activities, and provides with humongous potential growth and welfare increase. Some of them have reached an enormous scale and size, in terms of customers, revenues and market capitalisation, and an unprecedented economic and social relevance. Those platforms compete in global markets, interconnecting an enormous, and growing, number of users, and interacting with a myriad of companies ranging from traditional communications and media players to small, specialised companies.

The main, notorious, digital platforms are few global (not merely multi-national) companies, i.e., Amazon, Facebook, Netflix, Google, Apple, and Microsoft, which are patchily grouped and also known as GAFA, GAFAM, FAANG, MAMAA,[17] or more generally as "Big

---

[16] Co-regulation procedures are regulatory procedures participated in each phase by the recipients of the rules and characterised by a formally equal relationship in which the consent of the recipient is an essential element of the rule itself.

[17] GAFA stands for Google, Apple, Facebook, Amazon; while GAFAM adds Microsoft to the group; and FAANG reshuffles the order and substitutes Microsoft with

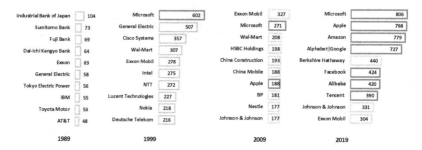

1989		1999		2009		2019	
Industrial Bank of Japan	104	Microsoft	602	Exxon Mobil	327	Microsoft	806
Sumitomo Bank	73	General Electric	507	Microsoft	271	Apple	798
Fuji Bank	69	Cisco Systems	357	Wal-Mart	208	Amazon	779
Dai-Ichi Kangyo Bank	64	Wal-Mart	307	HSBC Holdings	198	Alphabet|Google	727
Exxon	63	Exxon Mobil	278	China Construction	193	Berkshire Hathaway	440
General Electric	58	Intel	275	China Mobile	188	Facebook	424
Tokyo Electric Power	56	NTT	272	Apple	188	Alibaba	420
IBM	55	Lucent Technologies	227	BP	181	Tencent	390
Toyota Motor	53	Nokia	218	Nestle	177	Johnson & Johnson	331
AT&T	48	Deutsche Telekom	216	Johnson & Johnson	177	Exxon Mobil	304

Fig. 1.2   World top-ten companies by market capitalisation *(bn USD)*

Techs".[18] All of them, but Netflix, are among the global top 10 leading companies in 2019, in terms of market capitalisation, along with the Chinese platforms Alibaba and Tencent (see Fig. 1.2). The evolution in time of market capitalisation global ranking clearly shows the digital revolution process and that "Digital capitalism is the capitalism of the twenty-first century". In 1989 no digital platforms were included in the top 10 companies and only two ICT company, IBM and AT&T, hit the bottom part of the ranking.[19] In 1999, Microsoft was the only digital player in the top ten, although at the first place and quite a few ICT companies were included (i.e., Cisco, Intel, NTT Docomo, Lucent, Nokia, and Deutsche Telekom). In 2009, Apple joins Microsoft in the top ten along with only one ICT company (i.e., China Mobile). Instead in 2019, 7 out of the top 8 companies are digital platforms: all the USA GAFAM/MAMAA plus the two Chinese digital platforms.

Platforms' market capitalisation matches their market success, in terms of users and revenues. Indeed, Big Techs have been extensively rewarded and chosen by consumers because of their innovative services and ability

Netflix. Recently, the maternal-sounding acronym MAMAA has been created: it stands for Meta (the new Facebook's parent company), Amazon, Microsoft, Apple and Alphabet (Google's parent company).

[18] Big Techs have somehow replaced the so-called "Big Oil", that is oil very large multi-national companies (Exxon Mobil, BP, Gazprom, PetroChina and Royal Dutch Shell), as the capitalistic giants from the collective imaginary, and also from the top of the USA NASDAQ stock index.

[19] https://www.funalysis.net/economy-times-are-changing-world-top-20-companies-by-market-capitalization-in-1989-and-2019; https://www.cnbc.com/2014/04/29/what-a-difference-25-years-makes.html.

to meet consumers' preferences and needs, yet they also gained a tangible power to influence markets, competitive dynamics, and consumers' welfare. With time, two opposite economic and policy visions emerged about Big Techs' impact on market competition, i.e.,:

- platforms are (quasi) natural monopolies, because of economies of scale and scope, the direct and indirect network effects and the essential (data) assets they benefit, implying the need of a regulation and/or a competition policy approach similar to (other) network industries; or
- there is adequate (potential) competition in the market(s), mainly for the market(s),[20] as market power in digital world is temporary, because incumbent companies are subject to Schumpeterian displacement by more innovative new entrants (as it was the case for Myspace overtaken by Facebook, Yahoo by Google, Netscape by Microsoft Explorer).

Probably both these 'extreme' visions suffer some forms of path dependency, i.e., both are based on incremental and marginal extension of the economic thinking and policy approaches adopted for traditional network industries. In Sect. 5, both these positions and their arguments will be explored, describing why digital platforms economics seem to be leading to market concentration, what are the sources of big techs' market power, how that differs from "traditional" network industries' market power, and what could be a balanced policy strategy to address economic and competitive concerns.

An acceleration in the policy debate about regulation of digital markets occurred when it became evident that a light-touch policy approach to protect innovation must be balanced with the risk that unregulated markets and companies could lead to an excessive, maybe permanent, concentration of market power and possibly to consumers' harm. Indeed, also the most libertarian part of public opinion, seeing the internet as

---

[20] Competition for the market can refer either to (a) the allocation of monopoly right via a competitive tender process, or (as in this case) to (b) definition of new dominant standards or business models tending to a monopoly market structure, and usually associated with the process of innovation that brings new displacing technologies to market. See Geroski (2003).

a place of individual freedom to be preserved and therefore not suscep-tible of public regulation, progressively abandoned that romantic vision as it was no longer reflecting the changes occurred in the web: tran-sitioning from an almost atomistic decentralised system to a strong centralised one in the virtual hands of few global platforms.

As it usually happens in (disruptively) evolving market context, compe-tition law enforcement took the lead on public intervention, mainly because of its enforcement flexibility and ability to adapt to new market circumstances. The most relevant competition law cases for big tech at EU level, over the last years, concerned cases of abuse of dominant posi-tion (under Articles 102 TFEU): 3 subsequent cases involving Google, i.e., Search Shopping (2017), Android (2018), AdSense (2019) and one case involving Amazon about e-book 2 (2017) and ongoing investi-gations about Google, Amazon, Apple and Facebook. Moreover, still very relevant were few mergers' cases, e.g., Facebook/WhatsApp (2014), Microsoft /LinkedIn (2016)—see box 1.2.

Box 1.2 BIG Techs' main competition law cases in EU

The European Commission has investigated during the last years some anti-competitive practices implemented by Google imposing overall fines for more than 8 billion euros. In Google Search Shop-ping (2017) Google has abused its dominant position in the market for general search services and the market for comparison shopping services by giving advantage to own comparison-shopping service. Google held a dominant position in the search engine market, and according to EC has systematically emphasised the priority of its own comparison-shopping service, placing it in the first place within the search results (which are statistically the most "clicked" ones). Furthermore, the Commission claimed that competitors' purchase comparison services, which appear in Google's search results based on certain algorithms, have been downgraded. In Google Android (2018) Google was fined for abuse of dominant position in the markets for general Internet search services (search engine), licens-able smart mobile operating systems and app stores for the Android mobile operating system. According to EU Commission, Google would have forced the producers of the mobile devices to pre-install

Google search App and browser apps (Chrome) as a condition for licensing Play Store (the Google application to download and install apps), thereby engaging in anti-competitive tying. Moreover, Google made payments conditional on exclusive pre-installation of Google Search and imposed to manufacturers, wishing to pre-install Google apps, not to use competing Android operating systems. The Google AdSense case (2019) dealt with an abuse of a dominant position in online search advertising intermediation. AdSense for Search works as an advertising brokerage platform in search engines, intermediating between advertisers and "publisher" websites. Firstly, an exclusivity clause was imposed to publishers, preventing competitors from inserting competing search advertisements on their Google search results pages. Secondly a preferential placement clause was imposed to publishers, aimed to guarantee Google a minimum number of its own ads placed in the most visible spaces in the search results page, thus enjoying an illicit competitive advantage on competitors. Finally, Google imposed a control on how competitors' advertising would have displayed. In June 2021, the EU Commission has opened an additional investigation into Google's conducts favouring its own online display ads tech services in the so-called ad tech supply chain, notably imposing obligations to use its own services in order purchase and serve online display ads on YouTube, and restricting third-party access (by advertisers, publishers, or competitors) to data about users' identity or users' behaviour, reserving such data for its own use.

The Amazon E-books MFN case (2017) concerned the e-books market (where Amazon had a market share above 70%) and namely Amazon's distribution agreements with e-book publishers imposing retail price subject to the Most Favoured-Nation (MFN) clause.[21] The MFN clause consisted in an obligation for publishers to offer Amazon similar (or better) terms and conditions as those offered to its competitors and to inform Amazon about more favourable

---

[21] MFN—i.e., imposing to merchants a higher direct price compared to the one applied via the intermediary—is in general quite relevant for digital platforms.

or alternative terms given to Amazon's competitors. The Commission closed the investigation in May 2017 by accepting Amazon commitments not to enforce MFN clauses and any clauses related to inform Amazon about terms and conditions offered to competitors. It should be mentioned that in 2019 the European Commission opened an additional investigation aimed to assess whether Amazon's use of data from independent retailers who sell on its marketplace is in breach of EU competition rules. The investigation relates to 'data interdependencies' between Amazon's third-party sales platform for independent sellers ("Amazon Marketplace") and Amazon's own e-commerce activities: for example the role of data in the selection of the winners of the "Buy Box"[22] and the impact of Amazon's potential use of competitively sensitive marketplace seller information on that selection, and whether the use of accumulated marketplace seller data by Amazon as a retailer affects competition, e.g., those data are at the basis allows a preferential treatment of its own products as retailer against independent users of its marketplace.

The EC carried out two landmark cases involving Microsoft. In Microsoft I (2004) the tech-company was found to have abused its dominant position by bundling its Windows Media Player software with the Windows operating system and by refusing to share interoperability information with competitors allowing them to develop programmes alternative to Microsoft's on the market for servers. Further, by engaging in this anti-competitive tying conduct, Microsoft managed to expand its market power while hampering competition on the media player relevant market. As a result, competitors (such as software developers, content providers and media companies) lacked incentives to develop competing media players and were artificially driven out of the market.

---

[22] The "Buy Box" is displayed prominently on Amazon and allows customers to add items from a specific retailer directly into their shopping carts. Winning the "Buy Box" seems key for marketplace sellers as a vast majority of transactions are done through it (about 90%).

Microsoft appealed the order of the EC mandating the provision of a version of its operating system without the Windows Media Player. The General Court upheld the Commission's decision by confirming that the Microsoft's practice was abusive according to four factors, namely: (i) the undertaking concerned was dominant in the market for the tying product; (ii) the conduct in question jeopardised competition; (iii) the tying product and the tied one belonged to different relevant markets at the time when the conduct took place; (iv) consumers were not given a choice to obtain only the tying product without the tied product. In Microsoft II (2010) the EC argued that by tying Internet Explorer web browser with the dominant Windows operating system, the platform abused its market power. By hampering competition through an artificial distribution advantage, the EC stressed that Microsoft managed to make its own web browser available on 90% of personal computers worldwide. The EC finally accepted commitments from the company to provide consumers and original equipment manufacturers with the opportunity to install competing web browsers pursuant under Article 9(1) of Regulation 1/2003. In 2013 Microsoft was fined € 561 million for failing to comply with such commitments. In June 2020 the EC opened two investigations in order to assess whether Apple has infringed EU competition law. The first one concerns rules for developers on the distributions of apps via Apple's App Store, particularly (a) mandatory use of Apple's own proprietary in-app purchase system (IAP) and (b) restrictions on the ability of developers to inform iPhone and iPad's users of alternative purchasing possibilities outside of apps ("anti-steering provisions"). In April 2021 the EC has sent a statement of objection, describing its preliminary view about Apple's infringement of art 102 TFUE. The second case opened in 2020 deals with Apple Pay, which is a proprietary mobile payment solution on iPhones and iPads used to enable payments in merchants' apps, website, and also physical stores. The EC has concerns about art 101/102 infringements due to (a) Apple's terms and conditions for integrating Apple Pay in merchants' apps and website, as well as (b) limitations of access to the NFC "tap and go" functionality that is embedded on iOS mobile devices for payment in stores.

In June 2021 the EC opened an investigation into possible anti-competitive Facebook's leveraging of its market power from social networking services and online advertising to neighbouring markets, such as online classified ads ("Facebook marketplace"). In particular, according to the EC, Facebook may be using data obtained to classified ads providers for their ads on social network, in order to facilitate Facebook's marketplace to outcompete them. Furthermore, the embedding of Facebook's marketplace into its social network is under investigation as a possible form of anticompetitive tying. As for merger cases, Facebook/WhatsApp (2014) was investigated by the EU Commission in order to assessed the impact of the transaction on markets for (i) social networking services; (ii) consumer communications services; and (iii) online advertising services. Notably, as for social networking services the Commission assessment concerned how to consider social networks either as a separate market different from the consumer communications applications (IM and similar) or defining a unique market where the merging parties would compete. Investigation showed that their boundaries are continuously evolving as technologic evolution and usage profiles are driving to the convergence of both types of services: in any event the EC was of the opinion that the companies are, if anything, distant competitors. With respect to consumer communications services, the EC found that Facebook Messenger and WhatsApp are not close competitors and that consumers would continue to have a wide choice of alternative consumer communications apps after the transaction. Finally, most interestingly, with respect to online advertising the Commission concluded that, regardless whether Facebook would introduce advertising on WhatsApp and/or start collecting WhatsApp of user data for advertising purposes, the transaction raised no competition concerns. This is because, besides Facebook, a number of alternative providers would continue to offer targeted advertising after the transaction, and a large amount of internet user data that are valuable for advertising purposes are not within Facebook's exclusive control. The merger was cleared without commitments. It has to be noted that in 2017

Commission fined Facebook €110 million for having provided misleading information when notified the acquisition of WhatsApp in 2014, as it informed the Commission that it would be unable to establish reliable automated matching between Facebook users' accounts and WhatsApp users' accounts. Nevertheless, in August 2016, WhatsApp announced updates to its terms of service and privacy policy, including the possibility of linking WhatsApp users' phone numbers with Facebook users' identities.

As for the Microsoft/LinkedIn merger (2016), the EU Commission defined the relevant market for professional social networking services, for customer relationship management (CRM) software solutions and online advertising services (which was the only relevant product market where both Microsoft and LinkedIn were active). EC authorised the acquisition of LinkedIn from Microsoft under behavioural commitments aimed to address conglomerate effects and possible competition concerns. Namely, Microsoft agreed with the EU Commission that computer producers and distributors will be free not to install LinkedIn on Windows, the Microsoft operating system, and to remove it if it is pre-installed. Furthermore, the interoperability of other social media professionals with Office and all its connected programmes and interfaces must be guaranteed. Finally, the suppliers of the competing professional social networks must be further assured access to Microsoft Graph, the "tool" that allows (with the users' approval) software developers to create apps that can use personal data collected in the Microsoft cloud. Moreover, the EU Commission assessed for the first time the large concentration of users' data yet only in relation to online advertisement, finding that there were no competition concerns for advertising purposes, because (a) data protection rules may limit the ability of Microsoft and LinkedIn to process their dataset; (b) none of them granted third parties access to their database for advertising purposes; and (c) they were small actors in the online advertising market (compared to Google and Facebook, i.e., overall in between 5 –10%).

Another significant merger decision was the Microsoft/Skype (2011), concerning the sole acquisition of the latter by the former which was cleared in October 2011. The EC gauged the impact of the merger on two relevant markets: one involving enterprise communications and another limited to consumer's communications. As for horizontal effects on those markets, the transaction did not raise significant competitive concerns also with specific reference to calls and instant messaging via computers using Windows operating system. Moving to the potential conglomerate effect of the merger, the EC ruled out any serious competitive risk on the business communication market, if further deemed that the new entity would have not faced substantial incentives to harness Microsoft's market power to distort competition in its own favour. The EC found that even if the new entity engaged in bundling practices or tried to undermine interoperability to the detriment of competitors, this was unlikely to generate actual anti-competitive effects. Notably, the 85% market share enjoyed by the new combined entity was not considered crucial in the highly dynamic market of video communications, where most services were offered free of charge. Interestingly, this stance contrasts with the position endorsed by the EC in Microsoft I, where the company was found to restrict competition by strengthening its market power. In the same vein, network effects were not considered as a significant barrier to entry since competing operators could have easily set up alternative products thereby allowing consumers to switch provider very easily. The appeal of the decision brought by two competitors of Microsoft, Cisco Systems Inc. and Message net S.p.A., was dismissed by the General Court in 2014.

As for Facebook-Instagram merger (2012), the EU authorities did not consider it because the transaction did not fall within the turnover limits of the EU merger control. The merger was considered by the US FTC, and then approved with a non-public procedure in August 2012.

Nevertheless, competition law enforcement has been perceived by many to be too slow compared to digital market dynamics, and has been considered effective only for clear foreclosure cases where a dominant platform leverages its market power on another (downstream or upstream) market (i.e., all Google cases). Furthermore, antitrust intervention has been accused of not tackling the actual problems in digital markets, which are often not (only) those of market power. Moreover, in those antitrust cases, the definition of relevant markets is always quite problematic, given the conglomerate nature of the intermediaries, among more markets and more market's sides[23] and the peculiar features of digital economic transactions.[24]

Within the digital ecosystem 'economic transactions'[25] are at the same time multisided and centralised. This happens because (a) Big Techs work as markets' global and conglomerate intermediaries, and (b) dispersed information is gathered, managed, centralised, exploited, and appropriated as an economic good. These elements shape differently both supply and demand and, in turn, imply that each transaction does not affect a single "relevant market", but a number of markets. Therefore, the well-established antitrust notions of "dominant position", "market power", "abuse of dominance", "vertical integration", "marker failure", "pro-competitive regulation"—that were conceived and tailored for single transactions in a single relevant market—suffer from significant disruptions.

Furthermore, in many competition law cases in digital markets, it is problematic to identify a clear consumer harm, and antitrust intervention are very stretched in this sense, as the main economic characteristics of digital platforms, e.g. network effects, zero-price models and reduction of search and transaction costs, provide immediate and tangible benefits to consumers.

The standard notion of economic efficiency is typically measured in terms of (consumers) welfare in specific relevant markets, also when potential benefits from innovation are considered. This means that, typically, also dynamic efficiency and innovation are generally assessed with reference to specific relevant markets, with trade-offs involving current versus future economic agents (producers, sellers, and consumers), i.e., intergenerational efficiency and fairness consideration.

Economic efficiency in specific relevant markets—including the efficiency of specific institutional or organisational arrangements or private

---

[23] Bourreau and De Streel (2019); Hovenkamp (2021).

[24] Cabral, Haucap, Parker, Petropoulos, Valletti, and Van Alstyne (2021)

[25] Originally formulated by Commons (1924, 1930); and later reformulated by Williamson (1985, 2000).

orderings[26]—is then measured considering the "second best" outcomes relative to credible, counterfactual scenarios. The "Paretian" notion of economic efficiency implies that a market equilibrium is efficient if no other possible equilibrium may allow economic agents to improve their outcomes, without worsening the outcomes of any other. In each single relevant market, such dimension of efficiency is typically delimited by the lowest marginal costs of production–distribution, on the one side, and the lowest consumers' willingness to pay, on the other side. This implies that efficient market equilibria do generate "efficient exclusion": respectively inefficient producers-distributors having higher marginal costs, and "inefficient" consumers having a willingness to pay lower than marginal costs.

When economic transactions are multisided, as digital transactions are, they affect a few markets or market's sides at the same time,[27] thus affecting the way in which economic efficiency should be assessed. Indeed, positive externalities are generated across markets, whose transactions are possible only because of the intermediation of platforms (See Sect. 2.3).

The main point here is that in multisided transactions, intermediated by platforms, it is rather complex to define economic efficiency (and consequently what is an "efficient exclusion") relative to single relevant markets. For example, in some sides, marginal costs are zero (e.g., the production of information) or even the price paid by final users is zero (e.g., in many digital transactions where online contents or services are offered to consumers for free).

Digital platforms are sources of both economic efficiency (allowing transactions otherwise inhibited, i.e., resulting in "efficient inclusion") and inefficient economic power, generating "inefficient exclusion", as long as they maintain control over current and future transactions and reduce users' incentives (and even abilities in some case) to exit and to switch towards new entrants, when it would be advantageous for them to do so.[28] This entanglement can be defined "platforms (in)efficiency dilemma", in other words, how is it possible to keep the positive externalities generated and managed by platforms (including innovation patterns)

---

[26] Williamson (1985).

[27] Rochet and Tirole (2003, 2006); Armstrong (2006).

[28] Baker (2019).

yet disciplining their growing economic and bargaining power, thus maintaining a "workable competition" in the digital market society?

Based on these arguments, there has been a worldwide intense public policy debate on how to address this trade-off and, generally, to tackle the overall competitive and consumer issues in digital platform economy. Moreover, the policy debate have also focused on what policy tools, i.e., regulatory, antitrust, consumer protection and data protection, would be best suited to address those trade-offs concerning data and platforms economy (see box 6.2).

1.3 Big Techs and Online Information: The Pluralism Dilemma

The "platforms (in)efficiency dilemma" does not only affect economic efficiency, yet also may have other socially undesirable outcomes, such as negative impacts on freedom to speech, freedom to be heard, freedom to reach and to be reached in the digital informational sphere ("infosphere"[29]). Therefore, in the digital market society, there is also a crucial "platforms pluralism dilemma" (Sect. 7).

The spread of online platforms and, especially of social networks (included in the wider concept of the social media), has resulted in a transformation of the information system. Today's people daily information comprises both traditional editorial sources, either offline or online, and algorithmic source of information, such as those coming from news aggregator, search engines, and social networks. Moreover, also the information value chain has been subject to a profound change, allowing users to participate in the production and reproduction of content and, thereby, reducing the space for the intermediary role within the information system, which was traditionally played by newspaper, radio, and TV broadcasters.

In 2020, more than 50% of European used social networks as a source of information, while more than 80% got informed online. EU averages, as well as country distributions, are reported in Fig. 1.3 below.

In the digital market society there is a much larger availability of informative contents, due to the proliferation of "channels" on the supply

---

[29] Floridi (2014). The notion of "infosphere" is based and further build on the notion of "public sphere" elaborated by Habermas (1962)

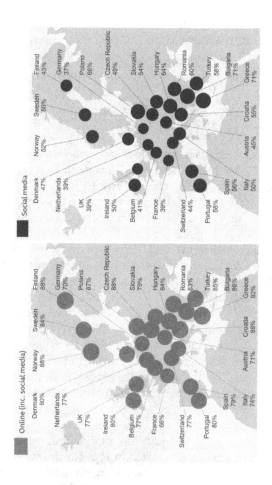

Fig. 1.3 Online and Social networks as source of news in 2020 (% of individuals) (*Source* Reuters Institute Digital News Report 2021)

side, also enriched by self-produced information content (which are made by the direct reconstructing of comments, news and information that do not only originate from journalistic sources but from a wide eclectic universe).[30] This has been considered by many thinkers the ideal world of free information and free speech, thus creating a pervasive "external" pluralism,[31] as a result of competition between alternative sources of information in the "free marketplace of ideas" (which in that theoretical framework is supposed to ultimately reveal "truth").[32]

This theoretical framework does not reflect the actual situation of the online information system. One of its main drawbacks is the high risk of information overload, that is an oversupply of information that consumers are not able to manage, thus hindering their conscious choices. That is why algorithmic sources of information are so used, as they address and resolve the digital information overload and efficiently select relevant information by perfectly discriminating and matching consumers (current) preferences on informative contents. So, the reduction of transaction and search costs also decreases time that consumers use to seek information. However, this unavoidably undermines pluralism, because algorithmic product-efficiency allow consumers to receive only the information they would like to receive, that is their own existing world representation. Instead, pluralism means precisely to be subject also to

---

[30] See AGCOM (2018).

[31] The external Media Pluralism's concept is based onto the proliferation of different source of information competing one against each other. This is different from the concept of Internal Media pluralism, which refers to the existence—within the same information system company—of a plurality of internal voices, e.g., journalists and editors with different ideas, background and so on. The latter is mainly used for publicly-owned broadcaster or Newspaper, providing for example a Public service and subject to a Public Service Contract.

[32] This is the very well-known "free marketplace of ideas" doctrine, developed more completely by Justice J. Holmes, a century ago, in the case *Abrams v. United States*, 250 U.S. 616 (1919), within its dissenting opinion, in the application of the First Amendment to the US Constitution. The First Amendment, among other things, governs the "freedom of speech, or of the press; or the right of people to assemble peacefully at meetings, and to petition the Government for redress of wrongs". According to Justice Holmes' dissenting opinion, "when men have realized that time has upset many fighting faiths, they may come to believe even more than they believe the very foundations of their own conduct that the ultimate good desired is better reached by free trade in ideas — that the best test of truth is the power of the thought to get itself accepted in the competition of the market, and that truth is the only ground upon which their wishes safely can be carried out".

informative content to which one might currently disagree. Efficient "content" matching, indeed, generates the unintended consequence, especially for search engines and social networks, to virtually cancel from the user's informational sphere any content that is not "likable" or anyhow that does not match with current user's profiling.

Moreover, the concept of external pluralism is based on an undistorted perception of demand, exactly as consumers' ability to discipline markets and produce an efficient allocation of resources is based on their rational, unbiased and fully informed choices. However, there is an endogenous confirmation bias in information consumption[33], reinforced exponentially by algorithmic profiling, which thus inhibits pluralism also on the demand side. In other words, this technical feature further exacerbates self-selection behaviours induced by cognitive biases such as *confirmation bias, groupthink preferences, anchoring effect* and so on.

As a growing number of citizens in Europe and over the world get informed through search engines and social networks, digital platforms' "efficient algorithmic matching" raises growing concerns on the nature and extent of online pluralism. At the same time, disinformation and misinformation strategies have succeeded in spreading falsehoods during elections and under the Covid19 pandemic, especially online.[34]

This process has been observed as the building of digital echo chambers and citizen polarisation, which might finally have a big negative impact on fundamental aspect of society and political systems.[35] Those outcomes are in most cases unintended by platforms, which have also developed and set internal policy governance to correct socially undesirable outcomes. However, this outcome is inherently linked to their specific business model, which is applied by platforms to all kind of products, information included.

In order to tackle the "platforms pluralism dilemma" and the spread of online disinformation strategies, the European Commission has launched in 2020, together with the Digital Markets Act proposal, a Digital Services Act, whose aim is to provide a new regulation towards a more transparent and accountable environment for digital users against illegal and harmful contents (Sect. 7).

---

[33] Sustein (2017).

[34] Vosoughi, Roy and Aral (2018).

[35] Sustein (2017).

Both "platforms' dilemmas" are based on the same economic mechanisms and commercial strategies: (a) the establishment of a business model based on implicit exchange between free services and data, in a multi-sided market context, and (b) the ability of reaching efficient outcomes similar to a perfect competition context, by internalising and exploiting information about preferences and willingness to pay of each customer.

These phenomena, jointly with indirect and direct network externalities, can lock users in an "information digital aftermarket", where platforms become gatekeepers, administrating consumers' information and selecting each user's goods and prices, thus becoming de facto "markets" (Sect. 5). This outcome may not be desirable from a competitive and social point of view, especially when markets and services affect information, public debates and other core democratic values and activities. In Sect. 7, we will ask whether in the digital market society, a specific new *right not to be disinformed* should be defined, in addition to the traditional right to inform and to get informed that shaped regulation over mainstream media in the past.

As we will see in the following (next Sect. 1.4 and Sects. 6 and 7) EU policy makers are approaching those issues and dilemmas in a coordinated and systemic fashion. This is very different from the "traditional" regulatory approach, which used to clearly differentiate rules and obligations for companies and consumers depending on whether their interactions took place: i.e., in the "market for goods", on one side, or in the "market for ideas", on the other side.[36] Indeed, the digitalisation has allowed different kind of services to be provided over many different networks by the same company in similar ways.[37] This *multimedia convergence*, magnified by global digital platforms, is at the core of digital economy and is also (seemingly) leading toward an efficient and coherent convergence of digital policy and regulatory frameworks.

---

[36] Coase (1974). According to Coase, the same consumers that in the market for goods is considered by policy maker as incredibly needy of protection from market power, cartels, misleading advertising, unfair practices, are instead considered completely rational, informed and self-empowered in the market for ideas.

[37] Manganelli and Nicita (2020), Sect. 8.1.

1.4   Regulating Digital Markets:
(Geo) Politics and Policymaking

In the early stages of their development, digital platforms embodied the positive side of a non-regulated world, where *laissez-faire* policies left 'checks and balances' to the market. This approach resulted in (a) pro-competitive entry of new, innovative and efficient actors into monopolistic or oligopolistic markets (such as the media and news markets, large retail distribution, book selling, taxi services and so on), and/or (b) creation of new products, services and markets. This disruption of "traditional" markets, companies and business models was perceived positively for long time by final users and also by policy makers (including antitrust enforcers around the world).

In the political arena, Silicon Valley became the core engine of digital capitalism, producing continuously momentous innovations, characterised by lower search and transaction costs, reduced barriers to access markets and service, and the possible realisation of a social enhancing sharing economy (see Sect. 2.4).

As described, with time, the global digital markets ended up being completely controlled by few US (and Chinese[38]) companies, (Fig. 1.2) enjoying an immense economic and social power. Their power is global, yet their legal and political roots are national, i.e., US-national. Indeed, Big Techs are deeply grounded in the US jurisdiction, which provided them with the economic, legal, and social context for their development. The EU has been very much at the periphery of the digital platform ecosystem's core.

Despite the unbalanced situation, EU digital policy choices were not guided by geopolitical consideration (or possibly in a minimal and residual part). EU (and EU national) policy actions have been based on their funding values, embodying a balanced relationship between market freedom and state intervention. Those same values have traditionally characterised competition policy and antitrust intervention, in a quite different fashion between the two sides of the Atlantic.[39]

---

[38] Chinese platform ecosystem is sub-global (for the moment), that is limited to China. That is on the other end of the ideological spectrum, where an autocratic regime fully controls platform companies and their power(s).

[39] Fox (2014). This remains true despite the so-called 'More Economic Approach' to Abuse of Dominance. See Communication from the Commission—Guidance on the

This situation, however, recently came to a drastic overhaul point. The original favour towards the digital platforms registered a dramatic change, even in the US. During the 2020 US presidential election, bipartisan political agendas moved towards claims for a stronger antitrust enforcement.[40] In 2020 President Trump issued an Executive Order against the alleged "online censorship" on social media, and the unchallenged economic power of "digital giants" (see Sect. 7). One democratic presidential candidate, Elisabeth Warren, in her campaign deeply focused on digital platforms, asking for stronger antitrust intervention, such as forced divesture, recalling the old antitrust intervention against Rockefeller's power.

Those kinds of concerns spurred proposals for reform both in the United States and in Europe, focusing also on data access regulations to reduce platform informational advantages.[41] In the United States, the Nadler and Cicilline Staff Report[42] warned that platforms have access to competitors' data, which gives them an unfair advantage in the market. They can keep many eyes on other businesses to identify potential competitors, buy out, copy, or cut off their competitive threats. The competitive advantage extends to the demand-side of the market. According to the same report, large platforms "can target advertising with scalpel-like precision, improve services and products through a better understanding of user engagement and preferences, and more quickly identify and exploit new business opportunities. This produces a self-reinforcing effect of drawing in more customers and generating more data." The report claims that large platforms benefit from returns to scale in information because they can update information for hundreds of millions of platform users at the same time while a small website reaches only a small percentage of online users. Data-driven revenue allows platforms to offer free goods, which gives them a further advantage in the marketplace.

The growing concern with large online platforms was bolstered, in the US, by the reintroduction of the neo-Brandeisian concept that large

---

Commission's enforcement priorities in applying Article 82 of the EC Treaty to abusive exclusionary conduct by dominant undertakings, OJ C 45, 24.2.2009, 7.

[40] Baker (2019).

[41] Glass, Gori and Nicita (2021).

[42] U.S. HoR, Subcommittee on Antitrust (2020).

companies have market and political power that could undermine competition and democracy.[43] Within this framework, it is recommended a list of screenings to assess whether a merger would cause a substantial lessening of competition, such as control over data and gatekeeper bottlenecks. Another recommendation concerns the extension of utility regulation tools such as access and non-discrimination obligation, as for example obligation to share data put on companies offering essential services.

In 2021, President Biden nominated Lina Khan as FTC Chairman, and Tim Wu, another heavy critical voice against Big Techs,[44] as expert in the National Economic Council with responsibility for Technology and Competition policy. The Biden administration seems at a turning point for competition policy towards Big Techs in the US. One of the issues under debate is whether antitrust law and competition policy should be redesigned to tackle the novelty of digital capitalism, thus providing governmental agencies and commissions (DoJ and FTC) and Courts with new powers and competencies, or whether, a change in the economic approach is needed under existing antitrust laws.[45] This approach has indeed put under revision some of the core antitrust principles outlined by the Chicago School,[46] that recently, within the digital market society, seems to have led to a substantial antitrust under enforcement, with particular reference to mergers clearance and monopolisation conducts.

In June 2021, the antitrust subcommittee of the Judiciary Committee of the US House of Representatives introduced five bills, jointly framing a new digital policy, comprising new antitrust enforcement powers and new regulatory provisions towards Big Techs, among those the "American Choice and Innovation Online Act",[47] the "Augmenting Compatibility

---

[43] Khan (2016, 2018). Shapiro (2019).

[44] Wu (2018).

[45] Baker (2019)

[46] Posner (2001); Bork (1978); and other eminent scholars and judges.

[47] H.R. 3816, to provide that certain discriminatory conduct by covered platforms shall be unlawful.

and Competition by Enabling Service Switching (ACCESS) Act",[48] and the "Ending Platform Monopolies Act".[49]

The US policy followed the EU proposals, advanced in December 2020, concerning a new regulation for Big Techs (and few other digital platforms), named as "gatekeepers", the Digital Markets Act (DMA)[50] (Sect. 6). A similar approach has been adopted in the UK, with the CMA Advice of the Digital Markets Taskforce.[51]

An overall global attention (finally matching the global nature and dimension of digital markets) emerged formally also in a recent G7 Ministerial Declaration: "By working together, including in existing international and multilateral fora, we can find coherent and complementary ways to encourage competition and support innovation in digital markets".[52]

In that declaration is reflected the need for international coordination for digital public policies' development and implementation, where indeed a cooperative (and not competitive) geopolitical dimension is needed.

As said, digital public policy involves crucial economic entanglements between, on one side, fundamental rights for businesses and consumers, and the static and dynamic market value of platforms' services, which magnitude also depends on their size, availability of information and ability to "understand" consumers. Indeed, big techs are today leading the digital transformation and with a fair and effective public policy framework in place they could very well contribute to economic and social growth as well as welfare increase for the digital market society. To achieve this result, policy makers should define core functioning principles for digital markets, comprising fundamental digital rights, possibly consistent at global level. On the other side, global platforms must

---

[48] H.R. 3849, to promote competition, lower entry barriers, and reduce switching costs for consumers and businesses online.

[49] H.R. 3825, to promote competition and economic opportunity in digital markets by eliminating the conflicts of interest that arise from dominant online platforms' concurrent ownership or control of an online platform and certain other businesses.

[50] European Commission, Proposal for a Regulation on contestable and fair markets in the digital sector (Digital Markets Act), COM (2020) 842 final.

[51] CMA (2020) Advice of the Digital Markets Taskforce.

[52] In April 2021, the UK, Canada, France, Germany, Italy, Japan, the US and European Union have agreed to the G7 Digital and Technology Ministerial Declaration.

embrace those principles and engage in cooperative and transparent interactions with public bodies, also aimed to develop a real, enforceable (co)regulation.

Public policy does matter, even within the cyberspace, as public authorities are those ones in charge and responsible to determine a fair, balanced, and efficient equilibrium between private interest, public interest, and social welfare.

References

AGCOM. (2018). *Report on the consumption of information.*

Armstrong, M. (2006). Comp*etition in two-sided markets. Rand Journal of Economics, 37*(3), 668–691.

Baker, J. (2019). *The antitrust paradigm.*

BEREC. (2013). Report on the NRAs' regulatory capacity.

BEREC. (2016). *Report on OTT services* - BoR (16) 35.

Bork, R. H. (1978). *The antitrust paradox: A policy at war with itself.* Basic Books.

Bourreau, M., & De Streel, A. (2019). *Digital conglomerates and EU competition policy.* CERRE Policy Paper.

Cabral, L., Haucap, J., Parker, G., Petropoulos, G., Valletti, T., & Van Alstyne, M. (2021). *The EU Digital Markets Act.* JRC Report.

CMA. (2020). *Advice of the digital markets taskforce.*

Coase, R. (1974). *Market for goods and market for ideas. American Economic Review.*

Commons, J. R. (1924). *Legal foundations of capitalism.*

Commons, J. R. (1930). *Institutional economics.*

Crawford, G., Crémer, J., Dinielli, D., Fletcher, A., Heidhues, P., Schnitzer, M., Scott Morton, F., & Seim, K. (2021). *Fairness and Contestability in the Digital Markets Act.* Yale Digital Regulation Project, Policy Discussion Paper No. 3.

EU Commission. (2010). Communication on a digital agenda for Europe - COM (2010) 0245.

EU Commission. (2016a). *Communication on online platforms and the digital single market opportunities and challenges for Europe* - COM/2016/0288 final.

EU Commission. (2016b). Communication on connectivity for a competitive digital single market - Towards a European Gigabit Society - COM (2016) 587 final.

EU Commission. (2020). *Proposal for a regulation on contestable and fair markets in the digital sector* (Digital Markets Act) COM 842 final.

EU Commission. (2021). Digital Compass 2030 – The European way for the Digital Decade.

Evans D., & Schmalensee, R. (2016). *Matchmakers: The New Economics of Multisided*. Harvard Business Review Press.

Floridi, L. (2014). *The fourth revolution: How the infosphere is reshaping human reality*. OUP Oxford.

Fox, E. (2014). Monopolization and abuse of dominance: Why Europe is different. *The Antutrust Bulletin, 59*, 129–152.

Geroski, P. (2003). Competition in markets and competition for markets. *Journal of Industry, Competition and Trade, 3*, 151–166.

Glass, V., Gori, S., & Nicita, A. (2021). *Online platform dominance: A case for dynamic first viewer advantages*.

Habermas, J. (1962). *The structural transformation of the public sphere*. Polity Pr.

Holmes, J. (1919). *Abrams v. United States, 250* U.S. 616

Hovenkamp, H. (2021). *Antitrust and Platform Monopoly, 130*(8), 1952–2273.

Khan, L. (2016). *Amazon's antitrust paradox*. 126 Yale Law Journal.

Khan, L. (2018). *The ideological roots of America's market power problem*. 127 Yale Law Journal Forum 960.

Manganelli, A., & Nicita, A. (2020). *The governance of telecom markets*. Palgrave MacMillan.

OECD. (2009). Better regulation in Europe: An assessment of regulatory capacity in 15 member states of the European Union.

Polany, K. (1944). *The great transformation: The political and economic origins of our time*.

Posner, R. (2001). *Antitrust law*. University of Chicago Press.

Rochet, J. C., & Tirole, J. (2003). Platform competition in two-sided markets. *Journal of the European Economic Association, 1*(4), 990–1029.

Rochet, J. C., & Tirole, J. (2006). Two-sided markets: A progress report. *The RAND Journal of Economics, 37*(3), 645–667.

Schiller, D. (2000). *Digital capitalism. Networking the Global Market System*.

Schwab, K. (2016). *The fourth industrial revolution: What it means, how to respond*. World Economic Forum.

Shapiro, C. (2019). *Protecting competition in the American economy: Merger control*, Tech Titans, Labor Markets, 33 Journal of Economic Perspectives 69 .

Sunstein, C. (2017). *#republic: Divided democracy in the age of social media*. Princeton University Press.

U.S. HoR, Subcommittee on Antitrust. (2020). Nadler, J., & Cicilline, D. - *Investigation of Competition in Digital Markets*. Subcommittee on Antitrust Investigation of Competition in Digital Markets. Majority Staff Reports and Recommendations.

UN Resolution. (2015). *Transforming our world: The 2030 Agenda for Sustainable Development* adopted by the General Assembly.

Van DijcK, J., Poell, T., & De Waal, M. (2018). *The platofrm society*, OUP.

Vosoughi, S., Roy, D., & Aral, S. (2018). The spread of true and false news online. *Science, 359*, 1146–1151.

Williamson, O. (1985). *The economic institutions of capitalism*.

Williamson, O. (2000). The new institutional economics: Taking stock, looking ahead. *Journal of Economic Literature, 38*, 595–613.

Wu, T. (2018). *The curse of bigness: Antitrust in the new gilded age*. Columbia Global Reports.

PART I

The Evolution of Digital Markets and Digital Rights

CHAPTER 2

Digital Capitalism and the New Economy(ies)

Abstract Digital transformation has progressively transformed economic interactions and commerce. E-commerce began as mere trading in on-line shops, very much decentralised and combined with many additional off-line actions. From there the internet economy has taken several directions, resulting in a fluid and complex digital capitalism, very often shaped by new forms of intermediations. The most popular examples of such intermediation refer to models of multi-sided platforms, acting as "matchmakers" among different groups of users, where business models often involve (personal) data as a key economic asset. Other examples belong to the so-called sharing economy, which can take different forms, therefore requiring a diversified digital public policy.

Keywords E-commerce · Online intermediaries · (Two-sided) Platform economics · Sharing economy(ies)

2.1 The Evolution of e-Commerce

Digital transformation of commerce has been at the core of the overall digital transformation. The evolution of electronic commerce, a.k.a., e-commerce or e-sales, has created new ways to do business. Thanks

© The Author(s), under exclusive license to Springer Nature Switzerland AG 2022
A. Manganelli and A. Nicita, *Regulating Digital Markets*,
Palgrave Studies in Institutions, Economics and Law,
https://doi.org/10.1007/978-3-030-89388-0_2

to e-commerce new services and products have been developed and geographical markets have been broadened; most intermediary functions have been transformed or replaced; relationships between market actors, both on supply and demand sides, have been completely revamped. Indeed, e-commerce have also remodelled consumer's behaviours in terms of demand patterns, availability of information, and consumers' role in the economic transaction and even in the value chain. At macro level, electronic commerce has been both cause and effect of the ongoing shift towards a knowledge-based economy and has pushed towards markets globalisation and the prominence of technologies in everyday life.[1]

A commonly used definition of e-commerce refers to the sale or purchase of goods or services, conducted over computer networks by methods specifically designed for the purpose of receiving or placing orders.[2] Each product or service could theoretically be involved in an electronic sale, which precisely depends on the ordering method and not on the features of products or services. Of course, ordering methods, as well as payment modes or delivery channels, have been subject to digital transformation, which also made e-commerce itself subject to an ongoing evolution.

Today e-commerce may take place over a (a) dedicated Electronic Data Interchange (EDI), devoted to B2B, (b) over the Internet, for both B2B and B2C, or via (c) some combination of the two. EDI is a set of protocols and standards for the electronic exchange of digitised commercial information and documents among different business information systems, usually not requiring any human intervention.

Box 2.1 When the e-commerce was born

The origin of electronic commerce date back in the late seventies, when the Electronic Data Interchange (EDI) was developed. Typically, EDI was adopted for transactions between companies active in the same sector, yet at different levels in the value chain, e.g., large retailers and suppliers, in order to allow warehouses database to communicate with each other.

---

[1] OECD (1999).

[2] OECD (2019).

EDI was not internet based, simply because at that time there was no internet. So, EDI system was supported by dedicated telecommunications lines or small networks in order to interconnect companies that have agreed upon a specific governance of electronic transactions and information exchanges.

It is clear how EDI-Commerce was a costly business solution, adopted only by large companies, for business to business (B2B) electronic transactions. The digital transformation and the advent of internet and then the web changed completely the e-commerce scenario. First of all, also smaller companies started to engage in electronic transactions, and business to consumers (B2C) e-commerce started to spread out.

Currently EDI may also rely on online channels, however it is not an interactive system, which means that sellers and buyers cannot negotiate, but only accept the data terms of the transaction, whereas of course web-based e-commerce has become a proper virtual electronic marketplace, especially when the web 2.0 era took place.

Nowadays, e-commerce is mainly web-based, however the transaction cycle (i.e., advertising, delivery, payment) and the overall commercial relationship (i.e., communications, aftersales assistance, and aftermarket products) may vary consistently depending on what is traded and the merchants' business models. Therefore, other internet services (e.g., e-mails), "bricks-and-mortar" sites, phone and traditional postal services are still widely used. As well for payment modes, currently e-commerce transactions largely rely on electronic payment systems, but also other means of payment are still extensively used.

Indeed, today a web-based commercial transaction is the most widespread e-sales practice in terms of engaged enterprises' percentage: in 2020 the average percentage of EU enterprises making e-sales was 21%, among those companies 15% made electronic transactions via web and just 3% via EDI, while 3% used both channels.

However, looking at turnover, the percentage of companies' e-sales revenues from EDI-based transactions is still much higher than revenues originated by web-based transactions. In 2020 the percentage of e-commerce turnover of all the EU companies was 19,8% of their overall

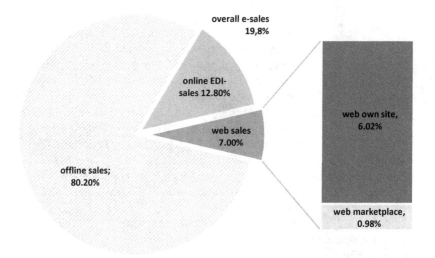

Fig. 2.1 Average source of turnover for EU enterprises in 2020 (*Source* EC digital scoreboard 2020)

turnover, broken down into 12,8% generated by EDI-type transactions and 7% generated by web sales (Fig. 2.1).

Starting from 8,6% in 2004, the percentage of e-commerce turnover has constantly increased in time due to innovation dynamics, first of all the outburst of mobile internet, which progressively enlarged the e-commerce scope (Fig. 2.2).

The 2020 turnover figure comes from a setting, quite differentiated country by country, ranging from 4,3% in Greece to 44% in Ireland. This variance depends on several elements, such as different deployment of fixed and mobile broadband networks and, above all, consumers' digital skills and enterprises' digital propensity (Fig. 2.3).

Looking at companies' size, it can be observed that large companies have a much greater propensity towards e-commerce: in 2020, 39% of large companies engaged in electronic sales, against less than 17,5% of small and medium enterprises (SMEs).[3] However, the trend of SMEs is

---

[3] SMEs comprise companies with 10–249 persons employed. Large enterprises comprise companies with 250 persons employed or more.

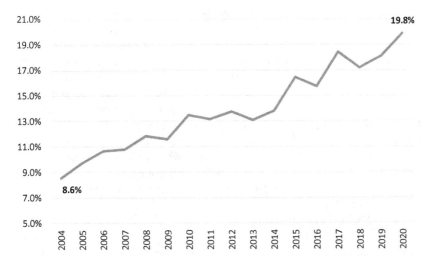

Fig. 2.2   Total electronic sales of EU enterprises as a % of total turnover (*Source* EC digital scoreboard 2020)

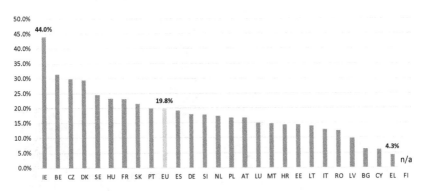

Fig. 2.3   Total e-sales by enterprise, 2020 (*Source* EU Digital Scoreboard 2020)

relatively growing, whereas large companies have had a flat trend in the last few years.

As a matter of fact, as long as the digital transformation continues to increase, small companies could access larger and larger geographical markets and thus an increasing number of new consumers. Indeed, e-commerce makes new domestic and international markets accessible to smaller businesses, which, generally speaking, are not so constrained by existing vertical relationships with retailers or salespersons. That's why it has been considered crucial to establish and consolidate an internal EU market for digital transactions, minimising the legal and economic barriers (see Sect. 3). Nonetheless, there are some technical and economic factors working as obstacles to engagement and expansion of SMEs online sales, e.g., the lack of digital competences and skilled employees; the use of standard internet business connectivity, whereas larger firms can have dedicated connectivity and *ad-hoc* contractual conditions.

In EU-27, enterprises that sell online are slowly yet constantly increasing their share of consumers' sales: in 2020, B2C web sales was around 11% for large enterprises and around 9,5% for SMEs (Fig. 2.4).

More recently, businesses are starting to become active on online marketplaces. As it will be better described in Sect. 2.3, online platforms' marketplaces can incredibly reduce transaction costs, improving sellers' visibility and capacity to access new markets and reach new consumers and thus completely unlock their growth potentialities. Nevertheless, looking

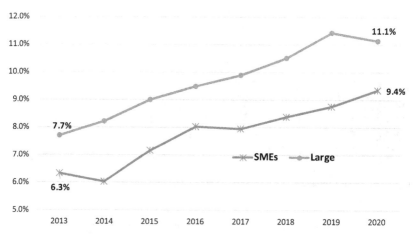

Fig. 2.4 Enterprises exploiting B2C web sales, by size (SMEs, Large) (*Source* EC digital scoreboard 2020)

at companies' turnover in 2020, the EU average of web sales via market-places summed up to only 14%, against 86% gained via own website or apps. This outcome comes from a very differentiated country distribution ranging from 35% revenue from marketplaces in Bulgaria to 4% in Hungary (Fig. 2.5).

On the end-users' side, the upward trend in e-commerce is evident. In 2020, around 63% of EU individuals ordered goods and services online and 23% sold goods or services online in C2C relationships, for example by means of online auctions or marketplace (Fig. 2.6).

Furthermore, e-commerce subscription modes, implying a continuous provision of goods or services and recurring payments, are becoming prevalent in B2C markets, particularly for intangible products, such as audio-visual content or electronic services. This evolution made it very important for consumers to have a guarantee about the continuity of service also when travelling abroad (see Sect. 3.3 about "content portability" regulation). This model has started to be applied also to tangible goods by agreeing on discounted periodic purchases or even by means of permanently connected smart IoT devices that detect scarcity and

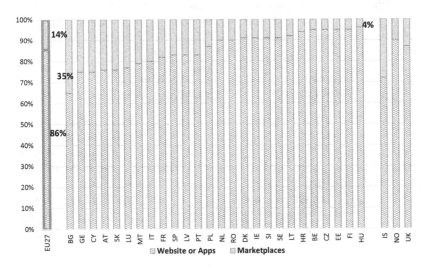

Fig. 2.5 Percentage of web sales in 2020 (*Source* EC digital scoreboard 2020)

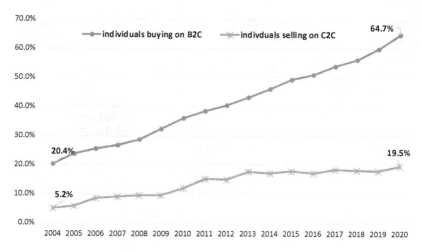

Fig. 2.6 EU end-users engaging in e-commerce

autonomously purchase products or its own supplies.[4] As a mere example, the Amazon Dash programme enables the automatic replenishment of supplies for connected devices like dishwashers, washing machines, printers, and water filters.

2.2 Internet Economics and Online Intermediaries

The expansion of e-commerce has enhanced globalisation of the economy and also its interactivity, connecting small and large businesses, and households and facilitating communications and business transactions. Namely, mobile technologies enabled consumers to conduct a range of commercial electronic activities, anytime and anywhere. Electronic commerce has also brought new organisational and business models, thus inducing, directly or indirectly, firms to assess their cost structure and competitive strategies and explore new possibilities.

---

[4] These are components of the so-called Internet of Things (IoT), that is a growing number of objects exchanging data and information by means of electronic communications technologies, with limited human interaction, and connected through and with the Internet network. See Sect. 7 in Manganelli, Nicita (2020).

It is evident how digital revolution has transformed commerce, deeply affecting some of its fundamental economic aspects, first of all consumers' trading behaviours, in relation to time, available information and places. Another crucial economic characteristic of electronic commerce is its impact on costs both on supply side, i.e., firms' productivity and distribution costs, and consumers sides, i.e., the reduction of transaction and search costs.[5]

As for the impact on prices, passing cost reductions to consumers is not an immediate outcome of e-commerce markets, yet it depends on the intensity of competition that e-sales brought into each specific market. Empirical studies shows that e-commerce placed downward pressure on prices in many markets, because of its impact on competition and innovation.[6]

Moreover, electronic commerce had an effect in reducing price dispersion, that is a variation in prices across sellers of the same service or product in the same market, due to the enhancement of consumers information and sellers' comparability. However, there are empirical analysis showing that online price dispersion is found to be significant and persistent also in the internet economy.[7] Indeed, the expansion of geographical market due to e-sales expansion could create a counterintuitive effect on price dispersion. This effect has decreased with the outbreak of digital platforms as the predominant digital business models, meaning that only the business model introduced by (global) digital platforms had a revolutionary effect on search costs and consumers' information availability.[8]

---

[5] Cfr. Brousseau and Curien (2007).

[6] Brown and Goolsbee (2002); Jo, Matsumura and Weinstein (2019).

[7] Baye, Morgan, Scholten (2004), which analyses detailed information on prices of 1000 items collected from a price comparison site. Baye et al. finds an average coefficient of variation of about 9% for goods being sold online. Gorodnichenko, Sheremirov, Talavera (2018), shows that although online prices change more frequently than offline prices, they nevertheless exhibit relatively high rigidity and considerable cross-sectional dispersion, and low sensitivity to predictable or unanticipated changes in demand conditions.

[8] Indeed, the easier explanation for price dispersion is due to consumers' imperfect information, i.e., not all consumers know who is the seller applying the lowest price. However, where imperfect information for consumers is introduced, in order to obtain a price dispersion equilibrium, one needs a framework where it is possible for consumer to obtain information of all current prices, like in a price comparison website (and not a sequential search, otherwise a natural outcome is not price dispersion, but monopoly pricing by sellers): Varian (1980). The main consequence is that both social and consumer welfare typically are decreasing with search costs.

As we will see in Sect. 2.3, e-commerce practices developed by online platforms (especially the tech giants) implies a massive price discrimination. However, this is an inherently different economic phenomenon, where a single seller offers different prices to different groups of buyers or in different geographical locations, while price dispersion refers to a variability of pricing from different sellers.

The reduction of information and search costs is a fundamental aspect of internet economics and played a central role also in the debate about economic disintermediation in electronic commerce.[9] Indeed, there was the idea that a widespread use of web could have led to a generalised "disintermediation", that is a displacement or elimination of market intermediaries, enabling direct trade between consumers and producers. This was supposed to happen due to costless access to network and perfect information about each economic actor, which would have made intermediaries redundant and their costs unjustified.[10]

Although e-commerce and web economy imply a trend towards disintermediation of some activities (e.g., streamlining of the distribution chain) this trend did not generalise. As a matter of fact, rather than eliminating intermediation, there has been a restructuring and redefinition of

---

[9] Interestingly, however, the mere occurrence of information gathering and search via the Internet is not enough to consider a transaction as e-commerce. The gathering of info on the web (especially on intermediaries' platforms) associated with a direct transaction (outside the web or outside the intermediary's platform) is actually a practice strongly opposed by online intermediaries, as it exploits the positive externalities of online service (reducing searching costs) without granting any benefits (transaction fee) to intermediaries. That's indeed a form a free riding, which could be however easily overcome by imposing a fee for the search service. This is of course often not convenient for a two-sided platform as the overall profits depends on the price structure (see Sect. 2.3); therefore platforms tend to use different economic tools, such as MFN clauses (imposing to merchants a higher direct price compared to the one applied via the intermediary). However, when there is a dominant market player, the MFN practice may well be an abusive conduct (abuse of dominant position) in competition law terms. See, for example, the recent 2020 CMA decision about an illicit agreement (Article 101 TFEU) for a MFN practice of a price comparison website in relation to home insurance products.

[10] The relationships between producers (or buyer/seller) and intermediaries are frequently interpreted as principal-agent relations. Due to opportunistic behaviours of the agent, the principal is confronted with agency costs, which are caused by informational problems like moral hazard (hidden or unverifiable action), adverse selection (hidden information) and hidden intentions. The agent must therefore have a comparative advantage in performing the task (such as a thorough information, implying a higher productive efficiency).

the intermediating functions in the web, first of all in order to establish trust and reduce risks involved in the electronic commerce (see Sect. 4.2) and to match atomistic suppliers with consumers, i.e., small companies and peer-to-peer activities (see Sect. 2.3).

Furthermore, in today's web sales rather than integrating intermediation upstream in the value chain, (some of) the largest players, i.e., online matchmaking platforms, intermediaries by nature, have integrated, vertically and horizontally, other segments of the value chain in their intermediation function (see market envelopment practices described in Sect. 5.1).

Online intermediaries' functions can be identified and distinguished into three main categories,[11] i.e., those ones that:

(a) facilitate the exchange process and "marketplace" function by creating 'immediacy' between sellers and buyers. In doing so, intermediaries bear some of the inventory risks of producers, reducing some transaction costs, and some search costs for consumers;

(b) gather, aggregate, and assess dispersed information which are relevant for the transaction (informational efficiency function of the market) and communicate relevant information to each part of the transaction, i.e., consumer preferences and willingness to pay, range of products available and their price. We will describe better this function in Sects. 2.3 and 5.3, in relation to large digital platforms; and

(c) reduce asymmetric information between the parties of the transaction and establish trust and reputation (neutral experienced third-party function), which is crucial in the online world where informational asymmetries are intensified because of the virtual nature of the transaction, implying an unavoidable physical distance.

These intermediary functions are often interdependent and sometimes partially overlapping, therefore there could be expected strong economies of scope and efficiency gains by jointly providing these three intermediation services rather than having them provided by three independent intermediaries. This is exactly what large digital platforms are doing.

---

[11] OECD (2019); OECD (1999).

2.3   (Two-Sided) Platform
Economics and Data Economy

The digital market society comprises nowadays a multitude of digital platforms, which have a broad scope of activities, e.g., online advertising, marketplace service, internet search engines, social media, creative contents aggregations and distribution, video-sharing, communications services, products price comparison, application distribution, payment system services, collaborative activities, etc.[12]

Online platforms have transformed the e-commerce landscape by matching sellers and buyers, inside and across borders, to facilitate online transactions. Indeed, platforms bring together a multitude of actors enabling a much wider scale and scope of goods and services profitably sold online, which might have been impossible offline or through individual companies' websites. In a recent book,[13] it is clearly showed the intrinsic novelty of the work of digital platforms as intermediaries: they are the "matchmakers", allowing individuals from different groups to meet up and benefit from the economic value created by this matching.

The term "online platform" in the context of e-commerce usually relates to a multi-sided marketplace that allows third-party sellers to interact with customers, without taking ownership of the products/services being offered.[14] However, online platforms often sell to customers as online retailers, too. Both modes are e-commerce, if the ordering happens online, irrespective of whether the seller is a third-party platform user or the platform provider.

A two or multi-sided market involves at least two groups of agents who interact via a platform. Of course, any market has both buyers and sellers, however there are specific additional features about those interactions that turn a market into a multi-sided one[15]:

(a) such a platform acts at least on the two different sides by selling two different products or services to two different groups of customers; in doing so,

---

[12] See EU Commission (2016); See also BEREC (2016).

[13] Evans and Schmalensee (2016).

[14] OECD (2019).

[15] See Filistrucchi, Geradin and van Damme (2013).

(b) it takes into account the fact that demand from at least one group of customers depends on demand from the other group of customers (implying no externalities for the platform); on the contrary,

(c) customers of the two groups do not take these indirect network effects into account (implying that there are externalities for buyers)[16]; moreover,

(d) customers on one side of the market are not able to pass it through completely to customers on the other side an increase in the price they are asked by the platform for the service.

There are mainly two stylised models of platforms: (A) non-transaction platforms, where there is not a transaction between subjects from groups on the two sides, e.g., service users and advertisers; and (B) transaction platforms, which allow or facilitate a transaction between the two sides, e.g., marketplace, auction sites. In different way, both kind of platforms have hugely impacted and transformed e-commerce, due to their ability to match different groups of consumers, therefore implementing and exerting a reduction of transaction and search costs, depending on the specific business model.

This economic and business model is not solely related to the web. Indeed, there have been (and still are) two-sided platforms operating, completely or partially, offline. Some examples are newspaper and free-to-air TV, interfacing readers/audience, on one side, and advertisers, on the other side; payment card system, interfacing consumers and merchants; travel agency, having travellers, on one side, and hotels or airlines, on the other; airports, interacting with air companies, shops, and travellers/buyers.

As for digital two-sided platforms, clear examples are those interfacing (a) sellers and buyers, i.e., auction sites (e.g., E-bay); marketplaces (e.g., Amazon); (b) merchant and payers, i.e., mobile payments (e.g., Paypal); (c) online "free" services' customers, such as people using search engine, online mapping, social media (e.g., users of Google, Facebook, etc.) and advertisers; (d) off-line service users and off-line service providers (e.g., Uber, Airbnb, Booking), where providers can be either professional

---

[16] This means that a two-sided platform is something different from a firm selling complementary products.

merchants, non-professional providers, or some combination of the two (see in this regard next Sect. 2.4).

A fundamental principle of two-sided platform economics is the one of "non-neutrality of the price structure", meaning that firms profits and consumer welfare are influenced not only by the price level but also, and primarily, by the price structure, i.e., the relative proportion of prices in the two sides and/or types of pricing (e.g., two-part tariff with a fixed component and a variable one).[17] Consequently, the size and growth of the platform depends on which side is relatively more valuable or where is more difficult to get individuals (i.e., people or companies) on board. Therefore, for example, a "free" transaction on one side of the market, e.g., customers that access to search engine or taxi online platforms, may increase rather than reduce the overall platform profits. Furthermore, a "free" transaction on one side may have an unclear effect on consumers' welfare, especially when the "free" service is coupled with an implicit non-monetary transaction, i.e., the implicit exchange of service against attention and/or personal data. Indeed, the basic common element of almost all digital platform business models is digital data and its valorisation as an economic good.

Online platforms, carrying out their activity, collect or have access to data (personal and non-personal) from those subjects they interface. Those data may originate from (a) a direct disclosure, e.g., in order to let the platform to (better) perform the matchmaking activity or provide (free) online services; or from (b) an indirect disclosure, e.g., while using online (free) services, yet not delivering that information to the platform but to other users via the platform. Both kind of disclosures may represent an implicit transaction against free or cheaper services,[18] yet remunerated by another side of the multi-sided market (the economic and market impact of this implicit transaction will be described at Sect. 5.3).

---

[17] See, for example, Rochet and Tirole (2006); Armstrong (2006); Filistrucchi, Geradin and van Damme (2013).

[18] Free or cheaper compared to a theoretical counterfactual scenario with no data implicitly exchanged and monetised.

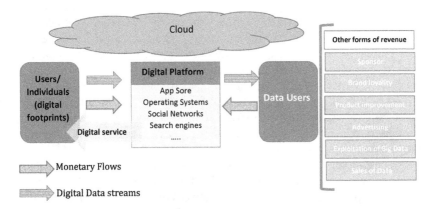

Fig. 2.7 Simplified representation of digital platforms two-sided market (*Source* AGCOM 2018)

Therefore, data and digital footprints[19] are indeed economic goods, and can be used by platforms to extract valuable information by profiling individual demand for services and products for all and each user, in terms of preferences, needs and willingness to pay, and therefore allowing forms of personalised advertising and forms of price and offer discrimination, ultimately increasing the probability and profitability of sales.

Platforms rely on profiling to monetise data by either using information directly, as retailers for online trade, or indirectly, mainly as recipients of targeted personalised advertising (see Fig. 2.7).

2.4 THE SHARING ECONOMY AND ITS (TOO) MANY FACES

Platforms have also promoted the exchange of goods and services in the so called "sharing economy". For instance, new kind of intermediation activities carried out by platforms have facilitated non-professional

---

[19] Digital footprints refer to a set of data originated by a web user's (person or company) activities, which can be traced and stored (according to privacy rules). Digital footprints can be (a) passive, that is composed of a user's web-browsing activity and information stored as cookies; or (b) active, that is released by a user on purpose in order to carry out some web activities, e.g., share information on social media, destination on online mapping and so on.

merchants to trade goods or services. Moreover, platforms have allowed the partitioning, allocation and exchange of goods and services' shares. As a matter of fact, partitioning and sharing, much more than a simple trading, require an incredible reduction of search, coordination, and transaction costs.

Indeed, as the words suggest, some form of resource sharing is always at the core of what is defined sharing economy. However, this locution is often used in an ambiguous way, as "sharing" can have different meanings and can be implemented in very different ways.

For example, the sharing economy is sometimes referred, in an exclusive way, to peer-to-peer (P2P) interactions (or C2C), either on a non-profit base (e.g., collaborative consumption) or involving an economic/monetary exchange. The P2P economy is related with the concepts of "prosumer" (being an individual both producing and consuming) and user-generated-content, when referred specifically to social media or video-sharing platforms. Another meaning of the sharing economy relies not only on the collaborative consumption, yet on the collaborative production, such as mass collaboration, crowd-based activity and wiki.[20]

Even classical commercial transactions between professional sellers and customers have been considered part of the sharing economy, as far as there is same partitioning of resources. The sharing economy can be understood to encompass transactions with a permanent transfer of ownership of a resource, such as trading brand new or second-hand goods, or trading exclusively some uses or rights of a certain good (e.g., partial use, temporary use), i.e., the so-called access economy. In any event, usually, both forms are implemented via online intermediary platforms, which create the matching and facilitate the exchange.

Often, it is not so clear-cut what is a P2P exchange, or a commercial transaction, as well as what is a "real" sharing economic model, rather than marketing strategy. As a mere example, the Airbnb is sometime described as a sharing economy platform for people that share the extra space in their homes; however, the space is almost always rented, not

---

[20] A wiki is a hypertext publication collaboratively edited and managed by its own audience directly using a web browser. A typical wiki contains multiple pages for the subjects or scope of the project and could be either open to the public or limited to use within an organisation for maintaining its internal knowledge base. See D.Tapscott, A.D. Williams (2006), Wikinomics: How Mass Collaboration Changes Everything.

shared, and Airbnb's listings are mostly owned by property management companies.

A satisfactory and comprehensive general definition of sharing economy is given for those activities having a combination of the following features[21]:

(a) largely market-based, i.e., the sharing economy creates markets that enable the exchange of goods and the emergence of new services, resulting in potentially higher level of economic activity;

(b) high-impact capital, i.e., the sharing economy opens new opportunities for assets, skills, time and money, to be used closer to their full capacity;

(c) crow-based "networks" rather than centralised institutions or "hierarchies", i.e., the supply of capital and labour comes from decentralised crowd of individuals rather than corporate or state aggregates; future exchange may be mediated by distributed crow-based marketplaces rather than by centralised third parties;

(d) blurring libs between the personal and the professional, i.e., the supply of labour and services often commercialises and scales peer-to-peer activities like giving someone a rife or landing money activities which used to be considered "personal";

(e) blurring lines between fully employed and casual labour, between independent and dependent employment, between work and leisure, i.e., many traditionally full-time jobs are supplanted by contract work that features a continuum of levels of time commitment, granularity, economic dependence, and entrepreneurship.

Notwithstanding, there is a profound theoretical problem in elaborating a comprehensive definition for "sharing economy". In facts, within the digital ecosystem, the sharing economy comprises a wide range of phenomena having as common features an evolution of property rights, that is inherently linked to the reduction of transaction costs and enhanced productive efficiency, caused by online intermediaries. However, these phenomena and the reduction of transaction costs can have completely different meanings and outcomes.

---

[21] Sundararajan (2016).

On one side, in a framework of collaborative production and/or consumption, a drastic reduction of transaction costs can facilitate the emergence of transactions associated with non-proprietary or collective uses (e.g., open collaboration or open-source economics[22]). On the other side, the reduction of transaction costs can determine a greater intensity of use of individual property rights, which may be fragmented, generating new exchange modes and new markets (e.g., the so-called "ubernomics"[23]).

The "sharing" can go in either direction, which are very different in terms of the property rights economic theory.[24] In the first case, we are facing the famous example of "commons", that is, common goods (common property owned by everyone or by no one) which have the characteristic of being legally non-excludable but also non-rival in terms of consumption, that is a public good.[25] In the second case, instead, the sharing takes place in a typical proprietary scheme, that is based on a legally exclusive use and, as such, exposed to rivalry. In this case, the sharing, meaning the partitioning of the bundle of rights associated to a specific good does not undermine the proprietary scheme. On the contrary, as said, it underlines a more intensive (and efficient) economic exertion of the asset and its property right.

The digital market society needs both forms of sharing. However, these two different phenomena should not be confused and associated into a single label 'sharing economy', especially by public authorities (policy makers and regulators). Indeed, the private ownership dimension of the "sharing economy" has effective market-based forms of protection and incentive, while non-proprietary forms, based on non-excludable and non-rival commons, may need some additional public intervention to regulate or facilitate coordination, e.g., eluding the "tragedy of

---

[22] First applied to the open-source software industry, this economic model is nowadays applied to a wide range of sectors. Some fundamental characteristics may include: (a) work or investment carried out without express expectation of return; (b) products or services produced through collaboration between users and developers; and (c) no direct individual ownership of the product or "company" itself.

[23] Gray (2016); Button (2020).

[24] Demsetz (1967); Demsetz (1998).

[25] Holmstrom (1990).

commons"[26] on the consumption side or incentivising the contribution to a merit good on the production side.

Many believed digital ecosystem could and should self-regulate without any external (public) intervention. This dimension, and its drastic evolution, about rules and digital ecosystem's legal ordering will be addressed in Sect. 4.1. However, also in the conceptualisation of the different kinds of digital intermediation and "sharing economies", it is evident that the digital ecosystem is characterised by pervasive asymmetries, in terms of information availability, economic and bargaining power, which always require public bodies' attention and supervision and, when necessary, a balanced intervention.

REFERENCES

Armstrong, M. (2006). Competition in two-sided markets. *Rand Journal of Economics, 37*(3), 668–691.

Baye, M., Morgan, J., & Scholten, P. (2004). Price dispersion in the small and in the large: Evidence form an internet price comparison site. *Journal of Industrial Economics, 52*(4), 463–496.

BEREC. (2016). *Report on OTT services* - BoR (16) 35.

Brousseau, E., & Curien, N. (2007). *Internet and digital economics: Principles.* Cambridge University Press.

Brown, J. R., & Goolsbee, A. D. (2002). Does the internet make markets more competitive? Evidence from the life insurance industry. *Journal of Political Economy, 110*(3), 481–507.

Button, K. (2020). *The "Ubernomics" of ridesourcing: The myths and the reality.* Transport Reviews, Vol. 40.

CMA. (2020). Case 50505.

Demsetz, H. (1967). Toward a theory of property rights. *American Economic Review, 57*(2), 347–359.

Demsetz, H. (1998). *Property rights.* The New Palgrave Dictionary of Economics and the Law, 144–155.

EU Commission. (2016). *Communication on online platforms and the digital single market opportunities and challenges for Europe* - COM/2016/0288 final.

Evans, D., & Schmalensee, R. (2016). *Matchmakers: The new economics of multisided.* Harvard Business Review Press.

---

[26] That is overconsumption of an open access resource caused by individual users acting independently, according to their own self-interest and contrary to the common good of all users. See the seminal work of Hardin (1968).

Filistrucchi, L., Geradin, D., & van Damme, E. (2013). Identifying two-sided markets. *World Competition, 36*(1), 33–59.

Gorodnichenko, Y., Sheremirov, V., & Talavera, O. (2018, December). Price Setting in Online Markets: Does IT Click? *Journal of the European Economic Association, 16*(6), 1764–1811.

Gray, B. (2016). *Ubernomics: How to create economic abundance and rise above the competition.*

Hardin, G. (1968). The tragedy of the commons. *Science, 162*(3859), 1243–1248.

Holmstrom, E. (1990). *Governing the commons: The evolution of institutions for collective action.* Cambridge University Press.

Jo, Y., Matsumura, M., & Weinstein D. (2019). *The impact of e-commerce on relative prices and welfare*, NBER working paper.

Manganelli, A., & Nicita, A. (2020). *The governance of telecom markets.* Palgrave MacMillan.

OECD. (1999). *The economic and social impact of electronic commerce: Preliminary Findings and Research Agenda.* OECD Publishing.

OECD. (2019). *Unpacking e-commerce: Business models.* OECD Publishing.

Rochet, J. C., & Tirole, J. (2006). Two-sided markets: A progress report. *The RAND Journal of Economics, 37*(3), 645–667.

Sundararajan, A. (2016). *The sharing economy.* MIT press.

Tapscott, D., & Williams, A. D. (2006). *Wikinomics: How mass collaboration changes everything.* Portfolio.

Varian, H. (1980). A model of sales. *The American Economic Review, 70*(4), 651–659.

CHAPTER 3

Building the EU Digital Single Market

Abstract Creating a European internal market is a fundamental objective of EU institutions. Consequently, the Digital Single Market (DSM) has been considered a far-reaching priority to boost EU digital economy and society. Given the global nature of digital transactions, in theory the DSM consolidation should not have encountered great obstacles, but in fact this was not the case. Fragmentation of rules at national level, as well as a widespread lack of consumers' trust on online transactions, especially when carried out across countries, represented relevant impediments, which EU policymakers had to progressively tackle. Building on the E-commerce Directive, which has facilitated the flourishing of e-commerce since 2000, a number of cross-border digital policies have been developed in the last years, among which geo-blocking and content portability regulations represent meaningful examples.

Keywords Digital Single Market · Cross-border e-commerce · Geo-blocking · Content portability

© The Author(s), under exclusive license to Springer Nature Switzerland AG 2022
A. Manganelli and A. Nicita, *Regulating Digital Markets*,
Palgrave Studies in Institutions, Economics and Law,
https://doi.org/10.1007/978-3-030-89388-0_3

3.1 The DSM and the E-Commerce Directive

Digital transformation and platform economy originated multi-faceted policy issues across all economy sectors with a global dimension. In this context, the development of differentiated and fragmented national digital public policies was a non-trivial risk. Furthermore, national policies did not tend to tackle the digital ecosystem in a systemic way, but to look at specific aspects in an isolated way, often by developing policies and regulatory solutions that just extended the traditional regulatory economics and consumer protection thinking to the new digital world.

In the last decade, the digital transformation has been approached by the European Commission defining and implementing periodic Digital Strategies aimed to create an internal digital market. In 2010 the European Commission adopted the "Digital Agenda for Europe (DAE)"[1] which was one of the 7 flagship initiatives of the Commission's Europe 2020 Strategy for smart, sustainable, and inclusive growth. This policy programme attempted to coordinate at EU level the public policies to ensure access to online activities.

The following Digital Single Market Strategy (DSM)[2] lunched in 2015 was aimed to specifically tackle the major obstacles to the development of EU cross-border e-commerce. This policy is today considered by the EU Commission as one of its top political priorities because it is strongly believed that its achievement is necessary to unlock all the potential benefits created by digital transformation and the evolution of e-commerce, thus sustaining the EU in the world economy.

The Digital Single Market can be defined as a market in which the free movement of persons, services and capital is ensured and where individuals and business can seamlessly access and engage in online activities under conditions of fair competition, and a high level of consumer and personal data protection, irrespective of their nationality or place of residence.

The three pillars of the DSM strategy are:

1. providing a better access for consumers and businesses to online goods and services across Europe by: (a) facilitating cross-border e-commerce; (b) limiting unjustified geo-blocking practices; (c)

---

[1] European Commission (2010).

[2] European Commission (2015).

modernising the EU copyright framework (cross-border content access); (d) protecting online consumer rights; and (e) reinforcing trust and security in digital services (cybersecurity) and in the handling of personal data (digital privacy);

2. creating the right conditions and a level playing field for digital networks and services to flourish by: (a) ensuring generalised connectivity; (b) incentivising investments for very high-capacity networks and accelerating 5G wireless roll-out; (c) reviewing the Audio-visual Media Service directive and adapting the existing rules to new models for content distribution; and (f) defining a transparent, open, and non-discriminatory regulatory context for online platforms, including the removal of illegal online contents.

3. maximising the growth potential of the European Digital Economy by: (a) addressing the barriers in the free flow of non-personal data in order to boost the data economy; (b) focusing on standards and interoperability; (c) supporting an inclusive digital society through the development ICT professionalism and public e-government plans.

Consistently with the DSM framework, in the last few years, the EU institutions have developed and implemented a set of coordinated policy actions approaching the digital transformation in a systemic way. Some of the policy actions based on the third pillars, i.e., the data strategy, are described in Sect. 6.2. The definition of the regulatory context for online platforms, which is a core element of this book, is addressed in Sects. 5, 6 and 7.[3] The DSM first pillar is at the base of quite a few policy actions related to elimination of legal and economic barriers within the EU and to consumer and data protection rules, which are described in this Sect. 3 and the following Sect. 4.

The fundamental piece of EU legislation, related to the first pillar, is the e-Commerce Directive,[4] dating back to the beginning of this century yet still in force. That directive mainly aims to remove obstacles

---

[3] For the other policy actions based on the second pillar, i.e., online connectivity, incentives to deployment of high-capacity networks and adaptation to digital transformation of the electronic communications and audio-visual media regulatory frameworks, see Manganelli and Nicita (2020)

[4] Directive 2000/31/EC on certain legal aspects of information society services, in particular electronic commerce, in the Internal Market.

in cross-border online services in the EU and to provide legal certainty for operating in the digital economy. The application of the e-Commerce Directive on the digital economy is broad, covering both B2C and B2B transactions as well as services provided free of charge, i.e., funded by advertising and sponsorship. The directive does not apply to traditional radio broadcasting, television broadcasting, which are instead covered by the Audio-visual Media Service Directive.[5]

The key principles of the e-Commerce Directive are: (a) freedom to provide online services (Article 3); and (b) freedom of establishment of online service providers within the EU territory (Article 4). The freedom to provide services across the EU Member States is enshrined into the internal market clause, which also ensures that providers of online services are subject to the law of the Member State in which they are established and not the law of the Member States where the service is accessible ("country of origin" principle). Member States can't restrict the freedom to provide online services except where such measures are necessary for protection of public health, public security, consumer protection. These measures must be proportionate and must be notified to the EU Commission, which control their compatibility with EU law.

In order to strive a trustworthy online environment, the e-Commerce Directive establishes harmonised rules concerning: (a) transparency and information requirements for online service providers (Article 5); (b) commercial communications (Article 6); (c) electronic contracts (Article 9 and following); and (d) limitations of liability of intermediary service providers (Article 12 and following).

Points (a), (b) and (c) generally relate to consumer protection rules applied to all online services (expanded in Sect. 4.3), while point (d) specifically focus on online intermediaries, regulating liability of service providers intermediary with the aim to eliminate market distortions and enhance the development of cross-border services. Considering the importance of online intermediaries in the digital economy (see Sect. 2.2), the harmonisation of national provisions concerning liability of Intermediary Service Providers (ISPs) represents a crucial step for the development of digital economy. Indeed, only a cross-country consistent

---

[5] Directive 2010/13/EU on the coordination of certain provisions laid down by law, regulation or administrative action in Member States concerning the provision of audio-visual media services, as amended by Directive 2018/1808/EU in view of changing market realities.

legislation can prevent and tackle illegal conducts such as infringement of copyright rules, spreading of illegal or harmful content, misrepresentations, incorrect or false information, and so on.

As for the current version of the e-Commerce directive, the general legal principle is that ISPs may be held liable only if they have some form of "control" over the content and information. In particular, the directive provides for a generally applicable system of specific liability exemptions on the basis of the activity carried out by ISPs: (A) mere conduit (Article 12); (B) caching (Article 13); and (C) hosting (Article 14).

As for (A), two types of mere conduit activities are expressly considered: (a_i) transmission of information provided by a recipient of the service in a communication network; and (a_{ii}) provision of internet access. By carrying out such activities, ISPs have a passive role, that is acting as a mere "carrier" of data provided by third parties via its network. When a mere conduit activity is performed, the e-Commerce Directive grants the ISP an objective exemption as long as the ISP: (1) does not initiate the transmission (i.e. the provider does not take the decision to carry out the transmission); (2) does not select the receiver of the transmission (i.e. when the ISP selects receivers as an automatic response to the request of the user initiating the transmission); (3) does not select or modify the information contained in the transmission. The liability exemption (B) refers to caching activities. Such activities can be generally defined as services aimed to avoid internet saturation. They are exempted insofar they consist of the automatic, intermediate, and temporary storage of data in local servers. Finally, as for (C), i.e., hosting, there is an exemption for services providing space on a server owned or leased for use by clients, as well as providing internet connectivity, typically in a data centre. ISPs will not be held liable for performing these hosting services if: (c_i) the provider does not have actual knowledge of the illegal activity or information and, as regarding claims for damages, is not aware of facts or circumstances from which the illegal activity or information is apparent; or (c_{ii}) the provider, upon obtaining such knowledge or awareness, acts expeditiously to remove or to disable access to the information.

That said, the directive purposely safeguards service providers from the obligation to check and control all information that flows through their networks because such obligation would be not possible or too burdensome for ISPs to perform (Article 15). However, ISPs have the obligation to communicate cases of suspected illegal activities to competent authorities.

As for the liability regime applying to intermediary service providers, the e-Commerce Directive was issued without having in mind current strong and dynamic platforms. That's why such provisions, which are so important for the function of the Digital Market Society, are currently under revision in order to better respond to its evolution. The Digital Services Act proposal,[6] which will be analysed in detail in Sect. 7.5, includes rules for online intermediary services, differentiating them according to the intermediary role, size, and impact in the digital ecosystem.

Nevertheless, up until now, by laying down a technology-neutral regulatory environment, the e-Commerce directive has facilitated the flourishing of platforms, and removed obstacles in cross-border online services, guaranteeing a smooth functioning of the digital ecosystem.

3.2   CROSS BORDER E-COMMERCE IN EUROPE

Cross-border e-commerce is based on fundamental principles of the EU Treaty adapted to the digital context: the creation of the single market, the free movement of goods, services, and persons, free competition, free enterprise initiative.[7] Geographic obstacles, blocks, or impediments within EU, as other forms of discrimination based on nationality or place of residence, are considered as contrary to the principles laid down in the EU Treaty.

Due to intensification of digital transformation, e-commerce has become more and more dynamic and differentiated. Some of the earlier barriers to e-commerce have been overcome because of new market actors, as online platforms, and new roles played by existing actors. Public policies played their part by increasingly looking at e-commerce barriers as crucial obstacles to remove in order to unlock the growth potentials of modern digital economies.[8] As a consequence, as seen in Sect. 2.1, the share of firms selling online has been constantly increasing, however many

---

[6] European Commission, Proposal for a Regulation on Single Market for Digital Services (Digital Service Act)—COM/2020/825 final.

[7] The freedom of establishment and the freedom to provide services guarantee mobility of businesses and professionals within the EU. Articles 26 (internal market), 49 to 55 (establishment) and 56 to 62 (services) of the Treaty on the Functioning of the European Union (TFEU).

[8] OECD (2019).

firms still face problems impeding them to further engage in e-commerce, especially by extending their e-sales in other EU countries, for example, cross-country complaints and disputes, high costs of intra EU-delivery and returns, limited language skills or differences in regulations. Similar symmetric obstacles on the demand side, such as augmented lack of trust and confidence, have refrained EU consumers from buying services and products from companies in other EU countries.

All these elements help explain why in 2019, only 8.9% of all EU companies and 21.1% of all EU consumers are engaging in cross-border intra-EU e-commerce. The percentage of companies selling abroad in EU have kept stable in the last few years and, although these figures are the result of a long-term increasing trend, they are not considered enough to fully exploit potential benefits of a large continental market. In 2015—when only 15.3% of consumers and 7.8% of companies was engaging in cross-border e-commerce—the EU estimated that consumers could have saved 11.7 billion euros per year if they could choose from a full range of EU goods and services when shopping online.[9]

Moreover, looking at the percentage of cross-border activities over the active online buyers and sellers, only 45% of companies and 35.2% of individuals engage in e-sales with other European countries. That figures even more clearly highlight how cross-border e-commerce is negatively influenced by specific cross-border impediments over and above those affecting e-commerce in a general way (Fig. 3.1).

This situation has been perceived as very problematic in light of the completion of the EU Digital Single Market. Therefore, in 2015, the EU institutions defined a few cornerstone actions, within the first pillar of the DSM strategy, aimed to eliminate those cross-border intra-EU barriers. The main actions undertaken are aimed to:

(a) enhance trust and confidence of consumers on online sales in general, which would have an even higher effect on cross-border sales, namely by (a_i) revising online consumer protection rules and (a_{ii}) reinforce trust and security in digital services and in the handling of personal data;
(b) facilitate cross-border online market dynamics, namely by achieving (b_i) affordable high-quality cross-border parcel delivery and (b_{ii})

---

[9] Cardona, Duch-Brown, Martens (2015).

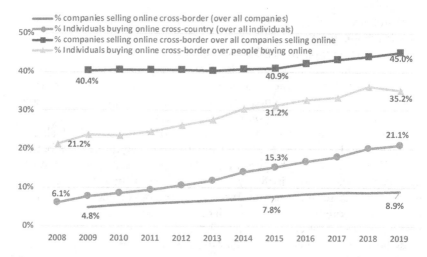

Fig. 3.1 Companies and individual engaging in cross-border e-commerce, over all companies and over those active for e-commerce (*Source* EC Digital Scoreboard 2020)

> reduced VAT-related compliance and administrative costs for cross-border online sales;
>
> (c) discipline the segmentation of online service and goods supply, by (c_i) preventing unjustified geo-blocking practices and (c_{ii}) improving cross-border service access for consumers thorough EU-wide portability of online content.

As for the consumers and data protection rules (a), those will be described in Sects. 4.2 and 4.3 as "fundamental" rights of the digital market society.

Cross-border parcel delivery services (b_i) is a crucial service for cross-border e-commerce because online sales of goods among different EU member states inevitably imply some services by a third-party parcel delivery service providers or vertically integrated online retailers.[10] In

[10] The importance of postal services for e-commerce is confirmed by the fact that the biggest retailers/marketplace platform, Amazon, has started a massive process of vertical integration with transport and logistic. In Italy, because of its logistic activity, Amazon had to take the authorisation of postal service provider, after that the Italian Telecom, Media, and Postal regulator, AGCOM, has sanctioned the company for abusive exercise of postal services. In the same line, in 2021, the Italian antitrust Authority (AGCM)

2018 EU cross-border prices were on average 3 to 5 times higher than domestic delivery prices for all products. Indeed, 62% of companies that wish to sell online identify high delivery costs as a problem. All these figures represent an evident obstacle for the development of cross border e-commerce and thus the consolidation of an EU Digital Single Market. For this reason, in 2018 a new regulation on cross-border parcel delivery services was issued,[11] with the objective to guarantee a higher transparency of prices and conditions, and thus a higher comparability, supported by the publication on an EU website of certain single-piece tariffs. Transparency and comparability are supposed to unlock positive competitive dynamic and downward pressure on prices. Moreover, the regulation enhances the national regulatory oversight over cross-border parcel delivery, as postal national regulatory authorities are asked to periodically collect information every year from parcel delivery companies and assess—for those services subject to a universal service obligation—whether prices are unreasonably high.

New EU e-commerce VAT rules, entered into force on July 2021, in order to eliminate some unproductive administrative costs on EU companies, especially on SMEs, engaging on cross-border online sales, and also to re-establish a regulatory level playing field with non-EU companies selling on EU markets. First, large online marketplaces are made responsible for ensuring VAT is collected on sales on their platforms, where they are made by companies in non-EU countries to EU consumers. Moreover, the existing VAT exemption for small sales (below 22 €) from non-EU sellers, which led to an unlevel playing field for EU companies, has been removed. Finally, in order to facilitate micro and small online businesses, a yearly VAT threshold (below 10 k€ per year) for cross-border sales has been established: under that threshold online sales to other EU countries are treated as domestic sales with VAT paid to their own tax administration.

---

sanctioned Amazon (more than 1.1 billion fine) for abuse of dominant position carried out by leveraging its market power from marketplace to logistic and transport activity markets, favouring its services against those of competitors. According to AGCM's findings, Amazon has tied the use of its logistic services to a set of crucial benefits to obtain visibility and better sales prospects on its marketplace, such as the "Prime" label.

[11] Regulation (EU) 2018/644 on cross-border parcel delivery services.

3.3   Removing Geo-Blocking
and Allowing Content Portability

One of the main set of impediments related to cross-border e-commerce concerns geo-blocking, that is a set of procedure restricting access to service and contents (or differentiating price and other conditions of provision) depending on the internet user's geographical position. The user's localisation is usually ascertained via different geolocation methodologies, such as IP address, GPS, RFID (Radio-frequency identification),[12] or via information autonomously provided by the potential customers, such as postal address, bank account details, and phone number.

There are different rationales underlying geo-blocking practices. Some of them are related to compliance with geographically differentiated rules, not disciplined at EU level, e.g., gambling, alcohol consumption or minor protection; whereas other rationales are related to cybersecurity schemes, such as blocking malicious traffic or fraud prevention. However, most geo-blocking practices are implemented because of commercial reasons, for example, geographically limited copyrights, especially for premium audio-visual media contents, as well as pure commercial strategies aimed to produce a commercial segmentation into the EU internal market.

Geo-blocking commercial practices are implemented by online sellers in several different ways, e.g., by limiting functionalities or access to online interface (mainly websites) from other EU countries; limiting access to services and goods (e.g., not shipping abroad or restricting the provision of pure electronic service to domestic customers) or discriminating forms of payment based on geographical aspects (e.g., not accepting credit card of a bank placed in another EU country).

In a 2015 assessment,[13] the EU commission found that 63% of EU retailers website did not let shoppers buy from another country, applying some form of geo-blocking practicing (Fig. 3.2).

---

[12] RFID is a technology of transmission, recognition, and validation of information at a distance, where the identification and exchange of information takes place via radio frequency. A variety of different cards use RFID, such as contactless or electronic access cards. In 2009, the European Commission issued a recommendation on the implementation of privacy and data protection principles in applications supported by RFID (2009/387/EC).

[13] European Commission (2016).

Fig. 3.2 What is allowed to EU cross-border customers by EU e-merchants, 2015 (*Source* EC 2016)

This represented such an incredibly high number against the objective of consolidating the DSM. Therefore, in 2018 a specific "geo-blocking" regulation[14] was adopted in order to break unjustified geographical barriers to online sales in the EU digital single market. In particular, the core principle of the EU Geo blocking Regulation is that online sellers must treat all EU consumers equally, avoiding unjustified discrimination, regardless of customers' nationality, place of residence or place of establishment in the internal market. The regulation applies to all companies (including online platforms) that sell goods or services within the EU territory to end-users.[15]

Geo-blocking regulation expressly disciplines three types of practices related to EU cross-border online customers that are considered unjustified per se, i.e.:

---

[14] Regulation (EU) 2018/302 on addressing unjustified geo-blocking and other forms of discrimination based on customers' nationality, place of residence or place of establishment within the internal market.

[15] Therefore, in principle, geo-blocking regulation does not cover B2B transactions. Nevertheless, those rules apply also to a B2B transaction, insofar it takes place on the basis of general contractual and access conditions (i.e., not individually negotiated) and the transaction is for the sole purpose of the company's own end-use (i.e., without the intention of re-selling, transformation, processing, renting or subcontracting).

(a) restriction of access to websites (Article 3) such as (a_i) being inhibited to access or use a website; (a_{ii}) being re-routed back to a country-specific website;

(b) restrictions to the conclusion of contracts related to online goods and services (Article 4) such as (b_i) not being allowed to buy physical goods without physical delivery (as the sellers is not anyway obliged to ship abroad); (b_{ii}) not being allowed to buy, or to buy at the same conditions as local customers, electronically supplied services or goods (e.g., purely online services: cloud services, antivirus, data warehousing or website hosting); (b_{iii}) implement geographically based price-discrimination on services provided in a specific physical location (e.g., concert tickets, museum tickets, rental of holiday accommodations, car rental services)[16];

(c) restrictions to usage of means of payment (Article 5), such as (c_i) having to pay with a debit or credit card from a certain country.[17]

The most significant exceptions to the geo-blocking regulation concerns retail financial services,[18] and audio-visual content provision and other copyright-protected contents that are electronically supplied. As for the provision of non-audio-visual content services (such as e-books, music streaming and downloading, software and videogames), providers are subject only to prohibitions related to Article 3, thus they cannot

---

[16] Such restrictions do not oblige companies to sell and apply price standardisation in all EU States and it is therefore possible to make specific offers/promotions for certain EU territories through different websites insofar companies make offers to certain specific groups of clients, such offers must be made on non-discriminatory basis.

[17] This does not impact the freedom of companies to freely choose which means of payment to accept. However, companies may not apply different conditions for a payment transaction when differential treatment is a result of the customer's nationality, place of residence or place of establishment, the location of the payment account, the place of establishment of the payment services provider or the place of issue of the payment instrument.

[18] There are rules in place concerning mortgages, opening a bank account and buying cross-border insurance.

geographically block or limit access to their online interfaces.[19] Audio-visual media services (AVMS) are instead entirely out of the scope of the geo-blocking regulation.

On this regard, from a 2019 survey,[20] more than 15% of web users resulted to have sought cross-border access to content in another EU country, mostly AVM content. This figure has almost doubled since 2015, showing a very drastic increasing trend. From this survey, AVM content is the most sought online product across EU countries and is the most subject to (licit) geo-blocking practices. Both facts are driven by premium audio-visual media contents, which have been excluded from application of general geo-blocking regulation in order not to completely sacrifice the economic interests of contents copyright holders, namely, to sell a geographically restricted commercial use of AVM content, in order to maximise its overall profits.

Indeed, regulation of geo-blocking practices in a copyrighted context must find a balance between conflicting interests, both deserving legal protection, i.e., efficient 'territorial management' of IPRs by copyright holders versus an open and competitive access to AVM service in the DSM by EU (cross-border) consumers. The EU approach to this complex policy trade-off comprises, on one side, the exclusion of audio-visual content provision and other copyright-protected content from the scope of geo-blocking regulation, on the other side, the adoption of other policy tools to balance consumers interest for a more open and more competitive EU digital single market. Those re-balancing policies are:

(a) an update of the audio-visual media services sector-specific discipline,[21] which governs EU-wide coordination of national legislation on all audio-visual media content, both (a_i) traditional TV broadcasting (linear services) and (a_{ii}) on-demand (non-linear) services, and on some aspects of (a_{iii}) video-sharing services. The revised directive generally addresses the digital transformation in the traditional 'television and audio-visual content delivery' sector

---

[19] Should providers of copyright protected contents engage in cross-border e-commerce, they cannot discriminate electronic payment means on geographical aspects (Article 5). The prohibition of Geographical restriction of access to services and goods under Article 4 do not apply at all.

[20] Flash Eurobarometer 477b (2019).

[21] Directive 2018/1808.

and facilitate cross-border access to audio-visual services also by promoting European works and preserving cultural diversity;

(b) an innovative regulation on cross-border portability of online contents,[22] allowing European consumers to use their online subscriptions to films, sports events, e-books, video games or music when travelling in other EU countries. In particular, it applies to (b_i) audio-visual media or other content provision services,[23] (b_{ii}) which are portable, that is technically accessible by subscribers regardless their location, (b_{iii}) lawfully[24] provided via the internet on a payment basis[25] (b_{iv}) to consumers officially resident in an EU Member State and temporarily present in another Member State.[26] Indeed, a substantial precondition for the portability enforcement is to ascertain a temporary presence of subscriber in another Member State, which in turn imply the ex-ante (when concluding the service contract) verification of the subscriber place of residence. The portability must be implemented in a non-discriminatory way, that is audio-visual media service provider must not in any way change, downgrade or differentiate price, quality, scope or quality of delivery of the online content service when used cross-border.

The importance of portability regulation must be read in the context of widespread development of new forms of audio-visual and music content consumption (e.g., via different devices and in different ways), which has drastically changed the characteristic of the demand for those contents. In 2016, before the regulation was enacted, 64% of Europeans used the internet to play or download games, images, films or music, and they did it increasingly through mobile devices. Indeed, one of the characteristics

---

[22] Regulation 2017/1128/EU, on cross-border portability of online content services in the internal market (Portability regulation).

[23] That is services having as main objective to provide access to copyrighted contents whether in a linear or non-linear mode.

[24] Compliant with the IPRs over the content.

[25] The regulation does not automatically apply to providers offering services on a free basis (such as the online services of public TV or radio broadcasters). However, free service providers can decide to be subject (opt-in) to the Portability Regulation.

[26] This must be carried out by using no more than two of the eleven verification criteria listed under Article 5 (i.e., identify card debit or credit card number billing address etc.).

of the connected digital market society is the possibility and propension to consume "anything anywhere".

Under an economic perspective, the portability regulation has tackled an inefficient setting within the relationship between Intellectual Property Rights (IPRs) and contracts, which restricted consumers interest without adding any additional benefit to copyright holders. In other words, content copyright rules address service providers, by restricting their commercial rights on a geographical base, e.g., what can be sold in country A by a service provider cannot be sold in country B by the same service provider. From an economic efficiency viewpoint, there is no reason why these restrictions should be transferred to the contractual relationship between that content service provider and its customers, who lawfully purchased in country A that content for their personal use, by restricting the use of that content in country B during a temporary stay.

Even considering that copyright holders may want to apply a geographical discrimination in order to differentiate the supply based on different average availability to pay in the different Member States,[27] this efficiency rationale would not in any way be impacted by the portability of the content. This is because the purchase of content by someone who is temporarily consuming the content in country B has been made according to the rules established in country A, and the price that has been paid reflects the average willingness to pay in the geographic area where the contract is executed. In other words, the geographical differentiation of downstream consumption does not affect at all the upstream IPRs geographical differentiation and its economic value.

The only justification for not allowing portability could possibly reside: (a) on any incremental cost for a geographical differentiated consumption; (b) on the possible *moral hazard*, or opportunism of users (who 'pretend' to be resident in the country with lower prices, or with a wider set of contents available, while finally consume the service in another country that is the real place of residence); (c) on possible actions of 'arbitrage

---

[27] In economic terms, the geographic differentiation of prices for homogeneous goods and services is often justified and considered efficient if demand is heterogeneous, such as there are different willingness to pay in different geographic areas. In this hypothesis, differentiated pricing, diverging from an average price, allow an efficient price discrimination, by allocating to different consumers with different willingness to pay a differentiated quantity of goods and services compared to the quantity that would have been allocated considering average prices.

piracy', purchasing in the country with lower price in order to unlawfully resell it at higher price in another country.

As for (a), that issue does not seem to be possible in the digital world, where marginal costs are close to zero as well as distribution costs. In any event, such an occurrence could be easily addressed by transferring that incremental cost to customers, even more strengthening price differentiation. There are several measures to prevent (b) opportunistic practices, e.g., when it comes to conditional access, it is easy to impose a maximum threshold of consumption in other countries, inhibiting the portability once that threshold has been reached.[28] Finally, with reference to (c), i.e., the relationship between geo-blocking and "arbitrage piracy", the incentives for its emergence and the rules to fight it are, in hindsight, totally independent from the portability.

In conclusion, content portability is not an obstacle for potential efficiency enhancing geographical discrimination, undertaken by copyright holders, although it could indirectly provide disincentives to grant exclusive territorial licences of rights to online content in each Member State. On the consumer side, content portability may well increase the perceived value of the content and, likely, be a take-off factor for demand in a consolidated DSM with enhanced mobility of European citizens.

These considerations are fully supported by a 2019 survey[29] (one year after the implementation of the new rules), which highlighted the benefits brought to European consumers by content portability. The survey shows that 41% of people who use the Internet to access content have a paid subscription to audio-visual content such as films, series or TV (excluding sports) and 26% to music, against, respectively, 20% for audiovisual content and 12% for music in 2015. According that survey, almost 50% of Europeans who have a free of charge or paid subscription for online content services have used it when visiting another EU country.

Finally, it should be worth underline again that all rules aimed to remove obstacles for the establishment and consolidation of the DSM

---

[28] Similar to the commercial settings deriving from the international roaming regulation—Regulation 531/2012 on roaming on public mobile communications networks within the Union. This regulation establishes a 'Roam-Like-At-Home' (RLAH) rule that mandated the end of retail roaming charges (differentiation of charges when travelling abroad), while also ensuring fair use and a sustainability policy, especially for data traffic, i.e., roaming data threshold.

[29] Flash Eurobarometer 477a (2019).

are also aimed to protect and empower EU consumers. An informed, confident, and empowered user (see Sect. 4.2) is what online markets, especially cross-border online markets, needs to expand and consolidate. As a matter of fact, those two objectives are synergic and both essential to build an effective set of fundamental rights in the digital market society.

REFERENCES

Cardona, M., Duch-Brown, N., & Martens B. (2015), *Consumer perceptions of (Cross-border) eCommerce in the EU Digital Single Market*. EC Joint Research Centre.

European Commission—COM/2020/825 final—*Proposal for a Regulation on a Single Market For Digital Services* (Digital Services Act).

European Commission. (2009). *Recommendation on the implementation of privacy and data protection principles in applications*, 2009/387/EC.

European Commission. (2010). Flagship initiatives of the Commission's Europe 2020 Strategy for smart, sustainable, and inclusive growth.

European Commission. (2015). Communication: A Digital Single Market Strategy for Europe - COM (2015) 92 final.

European Commission. (2016). *Geo-blocking practices in e-commerce*. Issues paper presenting initial findings of the e-commerce sector inquiry conducted by the Directorate-General for Competition, SWD 70 final.

Flash Eurobarometer 477a. (2019). *Accessing content online and cross-border portability of online content services*

Flash Eurobarometer 477b. (2019). *Cross-border access to online contents*.

Manganelli, A., & Nicita, A. (2020). *The Governance of telecom markets*. Palgrave Macmillan.

OECD. (2019). *Unpacking e-commerce: Business models*. OECD Publishing.

CHAPTER 4

Digital Fundamental Rights in the EU

Abstract The definition of digital rights has been an arduous task for policy makers, due to informational and institutional asymmetries vis à vis digital platforms, and to the fact that those platforms developed their own rules, and progressively built private legal orderings. Nevertheless, a public intervention turned out to be essential for a fair and effective functioning of the Digital Market Society, especially with regards to: consumer protection in e-commerce and online services; universal and non-discriminatory access to web and its contents; on-line privacy and data protection; and cybersecurity and safe use of the internet.

Keywords Digital fundamental rights · Internet legal ordering(s) · Consumer protection · Digital privacy

4.1   Internet Rules and Legal Order(s)

Today our activity, our identity and most our entire selves are web-based. The Web is an essential element of individual and collective participation in the society. Consequently, new fundamental and 'constitutional' rights for Internet users are what policy and regulatory debates have been focusing on for the last decade.

A. Manganelli and A. Nicita, *Regulating Digital Markets*, Palgrave Studies in Institutions, Economics and Law, https://doi.org/10.1007/978-3-030-89388-0_4

The European way for the digital market society is rooted in the EU primary law, notably the Treaty on European Union (TEU), the Treaty on the Functioning of the European Union (TFEU), the Charter of Fundamental Rights, by ensuring full respect of EU fundamental rights, e.g.: (a) Freedom of expression, including access to diverse, trustworthy and transparent information; (b) Freedom to set up and conduct a business online; (c) Protection of personal data and privacy, and right to be forgotten; (d) Protection of the intellectual creation of individuals in the online space; (e) Universal Access to internet services, in a secure and trusted online environment, where consumers are protected/empowered and asymmetries of powers are controlled. On this basis, in January 2022, the European Commission has proposed, to the EU Parliament and Council, a *Declaration on digital rights and principle*, aimed to guide the digital transformation, shaping it around the above EU values and fundamental rights and thus providing both to EU citizens, companies and policy makers with clear reference points about what should be digital rights and duties in the current and future digital ecosystem. The digital rights and principles into the declaration are grouped into 6 main themes: (i) putting people and their rights at the centre of digital transformation; (ii) supporting solidarity and inclusion (i.e., by granting to everyone access to internet, digital skills and digital public services); (iii) ensuring the freedom of choice online (i.e., by increasing fairness and transparency); (iv) fostering participation in the digital public space; (v) increasing safety, security and empowerment of individuals; and (vi) promoting the sustainability of the digital future (i.e., by aligning the digital and green transitions).[1]

Nevertheless, before talking about fundamental digital rights, it is necessary to talk about legal orders (or legal ordering). A legal order is a collection of norms, comprising (a) norms defining rights and obligations (primary rules), and also (b) meta-norms (secondary rules) on competences, powers and procedures to create, amend, and enforce primary rules. In other words, (a) deontic rules prescribing dos and don'ts in the web and (b) organisational rules about who or what define dos and don'ts, and who and how enforce them. Those secondary rules allow primary rules to "constitute a unity, and … have the same base of

---

[1] EU Commission (2021) and EU Commission (2022).

validity".[2] A legal order is therefore also a legal ordering, that is a set of coherent and ordered legal rules, which regulate (put into a socially desirable order) the life of a community, consistently with the Latin maxim *ubi societas ibi ius* (where there is a community, there [is] the law).

Legal orders are intuitively associated with States and public powers, because (a) the State has the highest and primary authority, yet circumscribed to a specific territory (State's Sovereignty), and (b) the State is a compulsory organisation, meaning that being a citizen and/or being subject to its rules are not individual choices (with some exception). Nevertheless, State's sovereignty and compulsoriness do not exclude the existence of other legal orders, according to the constitutional and legal pluralism doctrine.[3] Some of them, so-called derivative ones, derive their authority from the State itself, i.e., local public authorities, or supranational organisation established via international treaties. Some other are original legal orders, establishing and regulating communities on the ground of members' consensual agreement to belong to the same entity and not via authoritative powers.[4] Obviously, these private original legal orders discipline spaces of freedom that stand in between public legal rules (if there are), to which private entity and individuals must anyway be compliant with.

Membership based on consensus does not mean that private orderings cannot have an apparatus in charge of enforcing its (private) rules, on the contrary a dedicated institutional system differentiates legal rules (and legal orders) from social norms (and social orders). Differently from a legal rules' public enforcer, e.g., the government, a private enforcing apparatus cannot coerce members to hold a certain behaviour: private

---

[2] Kelsen and Paulson (1982). The essay reflects doctrines that Kelsen developed at greater length in his last full statement of the Pure Theory of Law (1960).

[3] Romano (2017).

[4] It is interesting to note that also the state doctrine based on social contract theories, hinges upon the consensual agreement between individual in order to create a political order. However, first of all, this is a *fictio iuris* as historically such contracts and agreement between all citizens never took place. Secondly, the social contract usually comprises both a *pactum unionis* (joining agreement between people) and a *pactum subjectionis* (subjection agreement of people to the political legal order). This second element, implying authoritative powers and impossibility to exit from that order, is absent to lawful private ordering (while can exist in unlawful order based on autonomous—unlawful—use of coercion like hierarchically structured criminal organisations).

legal orderings are inherently non-coercive. However, a private enforcer, applying the rules of a private community, can exclude a person from that community, when that person does not comply with its rules. For example, an association board can expel a member because of his repeated violations of the association statutory rules. Sometimes belonging to a certain community is the only (or most effective/easiest) way to satisfy a certain need, or to carry out a certain activity (e.g., bar association, basketball federation, and so on). Therefore, in those circumstances, community members are substantially subject to that legal ordering's private rules and sanctions, which become materially effective. It must be underlined that this effectiveness (besides the spontaneous respect of rules, which could be largely common) is based on the mentioned possibility to exclude, which effectiveness is however based onto public legal rules and thus onto State's authoritative power.[5]

Furthermore, private legal orders, as all collective and individual private entities, are not usually subject to territorial constraints, yet they clearly are subject to public authoritative powers according to where they are located (i.e., entity's place of establishment and/or members' place of residence). This imply that (a) a private entity can move from one country to another, changing place of residence/establishment, and therefore, to a certain extent, select what State's jurisdiction to be subject to (according to what is more convenient for the achievement of its objectives); and (b) a private entity can extend its activity and its private rules beyond the border of a State, implying that private entities may have to comply with different public rules, thus a cross-country (multinational) private legal order must either define a common set of rules that is lawful in each country interested or differentiate their rules country by country.

Looking specifically at Digital Market Society, there are several undefined nuances about its rules and its legal order(s). Who set rules to be applied in the Web, comprising users 'digital rights? Is there a private legal order? Is that private order subject to State law? What State?

In this regard, a significant part of the public opinion saw (and to a certain extent still sees) the Internet and the Web as a place of individual freedom to be preserved, under all circumstances, and, therefore, a locus

---

[5] As a matter of fact, the more a legal ordering is complex and well-structured (i.e., an element of society) and lasting over time, the more it tries to push, by lobbying, policy makers to include its main rules into State's law and therefore to have a more extensive and direct protection of those rules by the authoritative State's powers.

not to be subject to (external) public rules. Within this vision, Internet should have and has its own rules, establishing an independent legal order. Internet and the web were considered the newest world, a new space for a new age of discovery, a cyberspace, where new pioneers could find a new freedom, new rights and set new rules not affected by the old world's legacy, its powers, institutions and people.

Indeed, the main factual point here is that digital ecosystem has developed without a dedicated (public) regulation. This made it an ideal place for creativity and innovation, and indeed a precious and endless collection of ideas, contents, motivations and opportunities. When the internet and the web were atomistic decentralised system, rules were self-produced by the decentralised interaction of small actors, as for example the so called "netiquette", which was a custom set of rules enforced by the communities just by attaching stigma to violations.

This vision spontaneously tried to take the form of a *social contract*, via the "declaration of independence of cyberspace", which stated that: "Governments of the Industrial World, … you have no moral right to rule us, nor do you possess any methods of enforcement we have true reason to fear. … You do not know our culture, our ethics, or the unwritten codes that already provide our society more order than could be obtained by any of your impositions. … We are forming our own Social Contract. This governance will arise according to the conditions of our world, not yours. Our world is different".[6]

Soon after, this vision took also a neutral (not policy-based) technocratic approach, where algorithms and other coding system automatically affecting user's choices were considered an "objective source of law".[7] *"Our choice is not between 'regulation' and 'no regulation'. The code regulates. It implements values, or not. It enables freedoms, or disables them. It protects privacy, or promotes monitoring. People choose how the code does these things. People write the code. Thus the choice is not whether people will decide how cyberspace regulates. People—coders—will. The only choice is whether we collectively will have a role in their choice—and thus in determining how these values regulate—or whether collectively we will allow the coders to select our values for us. For here's the obvious point: when government steps aside,*

[6] Barlow (1996).

[7] Lessig (2000)

it's not as if nothing takes its place. It's not as if private interests have no interests; as if private interests don't have ends that they will then pursue."[8]

The "Declaration of Independence of Cyberspace" is a great ideal utopian yearning, but it is impossible to be translated into concrete terms. At the same time, the claim that computer code could represent an objective act of sovereignty remains an extremely vague and abstract idea, also raising concerns that code may be used to negate basic individual rights and freedoms.[9]

Of course, absent any public rule (or having ineffective public rules), the space of individual freedom would be almost unlimited in any society. However, with time, the absolute absence of public (State) rules and intervention would most likely result, as in biology and ethology, in a declination of the "law of the jungle", or of the "state of nature" where each self-interested entity (persons, companies) engages in a "war of all against all" (*bellum omnium contra omnes*).[10] Indeed, usually, private bodies are not on an equal footing, as asymmetric strength (physical or economic) is the normal setting in society and markets. As a matter of fact, public intervention, seeking a socially desirable fairness, exactly aims to counterbalance those asymmetries.

An asymmetric distribution of powers became evident also in the new digital world. The web was considered a place of freedom, assuming that once the public authority was excluded, there was no room for any private power. However, this romantic vision proved to be defective, when the web governance changed drastically: from a web composed of atomistic and decentralised actors to a strongly centralised system, where virtual networks and communities are centrally governed by large (global) web actors. Rules defined, contractually agreed with counterparts, and enforced in order to run their businesses, for example, platforms' terms of service's (ToS), started to become governance policies, e.g., policy about which content and users are allowed on social networks. Legally, these are contractual rules between users and providers, as well as rules governing the relationships between users, voluntary accepted by subscribing to service through an expression of free and informed consent. Substantially, those constitute community' rules set in a context of pervasive asymmetric

---

[8] Lessig (2006).

[9] Wu (2009).

[10] Hobbes (1651).

bargaining, market and social power, where platforms have the concrete possibility to define and enforce their ToS, which constitute what has been called "platform law".[11] That is platforms are not the recipient yet source of law: a rule-maker in a private legal ordering.[12]

To remain in a "social contract" narrative, this process might be seen as a Locke's "state of nature"[13] populated by atomistic users, morally bound by the internet "natural law", who then stipulate a Hobbesian social contract, which confers platforms absolute rule-making powers, by surrounding all rights and freedom (and not only those rights necessary to maintain the natural law as in Locke's theory). This creates a private legal ordering not subject to any (private or public) restraint, a virtual Leviathan (or few ones, dividing the cyberspace into a partition of quasi-sovereign spheres). Of course also this vision, in Hobbes' theory, is "legal fiction" (*fictio iuris*) aimed to provide an (ex-post) legal justification to the development of a *de facto* situation of unconstrained power. Such private legal ordering were (a) not subject (or not effectively subject) to public rules, because a limited regulatory capacity in the digital world[14]; and did (b) not need to rely on "traditional" public law-enforcement mechanisms, also with concern of the material (coercive) exclusion of a single user from the community, as platforms have the capacity (i.e., the material power) to exclude individuals from their community, because "in the cyberspace, virtual coercion is indeed effective".

As for the States' limited regulatory capacity (a), it hinges upon two main elements related to the relationship between public bodies and digital platforms: (a_i) a marked information asymmetry, due to the continuous and fast technological innovation that causes public bodies to always lag behind in terms of understanding digital market dynamics and platform internal technical functioning (i.e., platforms and algorithms as *black boxes*); (a_{ii}) the institutional design of public policy-making, which is

---

[11] Kaye (2018).

[12] Belli and Venturini (2016).

[13] Locke (1689). In Locke's vision, very differently from Hobbes', the state of nature is a "golden age", a state of "peace, goodwill, mutual assistance", a state of "perfect freedom" where each one is able to order his own life as he sees fit (so long as it does not violate another's natural rights).

[14] The concept of regulatory capacity is based onto the formal and substantive ability of public bodies to impose effective obligations, creating an efficient outcome in markets and society. For some examples, see BEREC (2013); OECD (2009).

traditionally set and implemented at national level, while digital platforms (and more generally digital actors) have a global nature, making it very difficult for regulators to both obtain information from them, and also to effectively design and enforce a regulatory framework applicable only to a subset of platforms' actions/users.[15]

As for (b), this is the most peculiar and interesting aspect of the digital private orderings. For example, the actual and effective power to directly exclude a user from a virtual community, or prevent him to use certain services, signals a legal order that does not need any public intervention. Moreover, this power—not ultimately based onto public intervention or rules—may effectively apply in transnational relationships extending beyond each single State's jurisdiction. So, the absence of public rules has an impact not only on the sphere of freedom left to private entities in the digital world (without considering private powers asymmetry), yet it gives the possibility to digital private legal orders to expand their virtual authoritative powers and apparatus.

Per se, this outcome does not violate the rule of law principle, as— under a legal (*de iure condito*) perspective—when a policy maker does not regulate, it means he chooses not to regulate, i.e., not regulating is itself a policy choice.[16]

A private order is never superseding a legal public ordering. Indeed, the State may (a) formally acknowledge the private legal ordering and even explicitly delegate it the governance of certain interactions taking place in some segments or partitions of markets and society, or (b) not considering those private rules and order as relevant, thus leaving spheres of freedom undisciplined by public rules.[17] In the past centuries, there were many examples of either explicit delegation to private orderings to perform certain rulemaking or enforcement tasks, in order to take advantage of their ability to understand and govern their own communities,[18]

---

[15] Goldsmith and Wu (2006).

[16] This is even more true for digital markets as there was an intended policy approach aimed to leave them unregulated, at least in the short term, in order to avoid the risk of a regulatory intervention that might hinder innovation in such fast-evolving markets.

[17] The State's legal order may also consider a private order as unlawful (i.e., criminal organisation) and contrast it with the legal use of force.

[18] MacCormick (1999).

or private regulatory determinations and enforcement mechanisms that have emerged in a variety of contexts in between State's rules.[19]

Either form is expression of constitutional and legal pluralism approach, where private legal orders can coexist with state legal orders. Nevertheless, these two forms of legal pluralism are inherently different, as the private entities' spheres of freedom take differentiated forms. Indeed, the rule of law and the principle of legality is based on the fundamental distinction between the sphere of "licit actions", where private subjects operate, and the sphere of "legitimate actions", where public subjects act. When private bodies are delegated by public powers to act in their behalf, they must act in the sphere of legitimate action, meaning that they can do only what the law entitle and empower them to do. Whereas, otherwise, private subjects can lawfully do what is not forbidden to them.

This implies that private entity's actions, absent any public delegation, have to be assessed in the underlying contractual relationship framework. Therefore, the absence of primary public rules, trying to pursue the public interest and fairness objectives, may result in an unconstrained exertion of economic and market power by the stronger part and the lack of protection for the weaker parts.

This outcome may in turn let emerge:

(a) Individual being subject to private rules, that they have contractually accepted, yet under an incredible asymmetric unbalance of informational and bargaining power; and

(b) a private service *de facto* transformed into an "essential (public) service" or a "service of general economic interest", necessary to exercise certain constitutionally protected rights, without any legal delegation or assignment of special rights.

As for (a), private ordering rules, as ToS, are unilaterally drafted standard contractual terms whose enforceability exclusively depends on the intermediary's actions. Such unilateral definition and implementation of contractual rules may carry undesirable consequences, in terms of fairness, depending on the asymmetric balance of private powers. To this end, the expression of consent to ToS becomes a fundamental action allowing

---

[19] Cafaggi (2004); Zumbansen (2013).

the intermediaries to deploy their private ordering, based on a contractual relation into which the individual is assumed to enter freely and fully informed. This outcome, however, "holds true only in the absence of any market failure that would undermine the fundamental propositions on which the freedom of contract rests".[20] It is therefore crucial the definition of consumers-users protection and empowerment rules, which (more than in a traditional market and society context) are fundamental rights of the digital market society ordering (see the following Sects. 4.2, 4.3 and 4.4).

As for (b), this may create a confusing overlapping between platforms' modes of action, located somewhere between the sphere of licit and the sphere of legitimate actions, and on their nature and objectives, i.e., public versus private. For example, the exclusion and interruption of the provision of a service for breach of contractual terms has been considered in light of constitutional rights protection, and not a mere contractual dispute between the parties.[21] Actually, the problem here is ultimately private power, in the meaning of market power, that is "a position of economic strength of an undertaking ... affording it the power to behave to an appreciable extent independently of its competitors, its customers and ultimately of the consumers".[22] This becomes clear when one considers that the exclusion from a platform having a small number of users and services could not possibly be considered a violation of individual fundamental rights. In other words, only when platforms' size and scope become similar to size and scope of markets and/or society, then their service can become somehow 'essential' and their rules somehow 'binding'. So, if the problem is market, economic and bargaining power, it is right to focus on rules, public rules, concerning undistorted and fair competition dynamics and consumers' empowerment, as the European policy maker is proposing (Sects. 5, 6 and 7), leaving platforms in a private sphere of licit behaviours, publicly regulated, and not endowing them with a "public service provider" status, which in the long term may

---

[20] Elkin-Koren (1997).

[21] In this regard, there are two conflicting decisions before Italian tribunals about Facebook's exclusion of far-right parties (i.e., Casa Pound and Forza Nuova) from its service.

[22] European Court of Justice, 13 February 1979, Case 85/76, Hoffmann-La Roche, para. 38.

well be a counterproductive element in establishing effective limits to their economic and market power.[23]

Within this context is blatantly evident that the public policy choice is not (any longer) between regulation or no regulation, yet the choice is between different kind of legal orders, private versus public (or a combination of the two), and namely the different extent and degree of the public intervention, and consequently the sphere of freedom left to private entities, which can be configured into power for few (platforms) and subjection for many (users).

Today, in fact, both the general opinion and policy makers have realised that some aspects of internet must be necessarily defined and regulated by public rules, as for example the protection of consumer, and platforms' market power. Moreover, consumers must be empowered in order to counterbalance and discipline the economic power of online platforms, and to move (again) toward a more decentralised functioning of the Digital Market Society.

More generally, some believe that public bodies should completely bring back all rules under their domains, while others would prefer a more balanced approach, in light of legal and constitutional pluralism,[24] where a global private legal order can coexist with state legal orders. The latter scenario is one where the public authority and the society can take advantage of platforms' ability to understand, foresee and govern their own communities within the digital market society. This may result in an effective, fair outcome, if policy makers manage to define (a) fundamental digital rights for users; (b) effective enforcement systems (e.g., by empowering regulators with adequate inspection and audit powers),[25] and (c) bring back authoritative powers closer to the State legal order, for example by enacting rules somehow including Internet Service Providers and telecom network operators, which have mostly a national dimension, in the platform service contractual relationship.

To go on within the *natural law* rhetoric, an adequate, effective and fair regulatory framework could transform virtual Leviathans (à la Hoobes) or tech Titans (à la Economist: "how to tame tech titans") into

---

[23] Srnicek (2017); More generally, Srnicek (2016).

[24] MacCormick (1999); Romano (2017).

[25] De Streel and Ledger (2020).

Giants, on which shoulders we could stand and make the future a bit less obscure.

4.2   Right to Access a Secure and Trusted Digital Ecosystem

A public intervention is crucial for a fair and effective functioning of the Digital Market Society digital ecosystem, especially in those contexts where private rules and private powers are pervasive. Internet users' rights represent the fundamental and constitutional bundle of rights of the Digital Market Society and are pivotal for building the EU Digital Single Market.

Those are, *inter alia*, internet users' rights related to (a) consumer protection in e-commerce and online services; (b) access to web and its contents (or generation and distribution of self-generated contents) in a universal and non-discriminatory way; (c) online privacy and data protection; and (d) a safe and secure networks and information systems (i.e., cybersecurity and cyber resilience).

As highlighted, end-user and consumer policies go beyond the mere protection of individual rights and get a systemic dimension. Empowered consumers, not impeded (endogenously or exogenously) in their free, rational, and informed choices, can (a) play a disciplining role in the market, by sanctioning with their choices "bad" companies or services, and (b) decide to remain subject to private rules, after a clear understanding and substantial consensual agreement, only if they will have a benefit from it, being the best guardians of their own interests.

Indeed, the centrality of consumers in economic theory originates from the idea that demand-side undistorted choices between alternative options is the ultimate force that disciplines companies' market power and introduces in the market appropriate incentives for firms. According to Adam Smith, "consumption is the only end and purpose of all production; and the interest of the producer ought to be attended to, only so far as it may be necessary for promoting that of the consumer".[26]

This conceptualisation holds within the *homo economicus* assumption, where both consumers and producers behave fully rationally and maximise their own utility. This is an ideal scenario: in reality consumers often

---

[26] Smith (1776).

happen to be unable to access relevant information, and even to assess their own (intertemporal) preferences in order to maximise their utility, because they are misled by bounded rationality, cognitive biases, and inertia.[27] This realistic scenario of consumers' limited rationality, in turn, often implies that the information provided by companies (even under legal obligations) does not really allow consumers to take a well-informed decision.

Moreover, the *homo economicus* paradigm is based onto consumers' perfect and complete information. In this ideal scenario, trust is not needed because perfect knowledge produces efficient anonymous exchanges. However, in a world of either incomplete information, or 'information overload' (which the web is often creating) market transactions need trust, which become a commodity. In this regard, Adam Smith also wrote that economic exchange is possible only if there is trust because "a handshake is a handshake".[28]

As a matter of fact, as described in Sect. 2.2, the conditions to boost electronic trading and to allow it to materialise a positive impact on the markets, largely hinge on the confidence and trust that businesses are able to create in their relations with their partners and customers, in terms both of (a) individual confidence toward specific sellers (e.g., the quality of what they are selling, their customer care, treatment of personal information and data) and (b) a systemic trust on the internet and web environment (i.e., confidence in the security of the network, of the electronic payment systems and so on).

Fostering confidence in electronic markets, particularly among consumers, is a crucial policy field. Different mechanisms could be developed in order to enhance trust: (a) some of those directly by the market itself, i.e., by neutral third-party intermediaries, P2P reviewers, price comparison website; and (b) some others by public policies, i.e., digital consumer protection, data protection, and cybersecurity.

During the last years, both types of mechanisms have been developed.

As for networks' security, at the end of 2020, the EC presented an update of the EU Cybersecurity Strategy, which covers the security of essential services, such as hospitals, energy grids and railways, and the

---

[27] Simon (1955); Thaler (1985); Akerlof and Schiller (2009); Allcott and Sunstein (2015).

[28] Smith (1759).

security of the quickly increasing number IoTs' objects. This strategy focuses on building collective capabilities to respond to major cyberattacks and sets the conditions to cooperate with partners around the world to ensure international security and stability in cyberspace. The main act of the strategy is the so-called NIS Directive,[29] that, for the first time, aims at ensuring a high safety level of digital network and information at European level. The online platforms providing 'marketplace' services (e.g., Amazon, e-Bay, etc.), search engines (e.g., Google, Yahoo, etc.) and the 'cloud computing' services must ensure the security of their infrastructure, and promptly report cyber-attacks to their systems and to the security of the data held by them. Similar obligations are imposed on operators in the energy, transport, and health sectors, as well as in the banking system, which will be identified, by a competent national authority, as "critical operators" providing essential services. The NIS directive also established the European Union Agency for Network and Information Security (ENISA), whose powers and competences have been reinforced in 2019[30] by the so-called Cybersecurity Act on ENISA and on information and communications technology cybersecurity certification.

In the Fig. 4.1 below, it is evident how the main negative events affecting digital consumers (i.e., virus, frauds, privacy violations) have been constantly decreasing in the last 10 years, however consumers' concerns and lack of trust have decreased less than proportionally.

To create a solid trust and self-confidence, online users should also be equipped with basic digital skills—which should become a fundamental right to be grant universally, in order to allow all people to fully participate in economic and societal activities of today and of tomorrow.[31]

Indeed, another crucial element for boosting digital transactions and DSM consolidation is digital literacy, i.e., abstract thinking and practical skills enabling the fruitful use and understanding of digital technologies, services, and interactions. Enhancing digital literacy is a direct consumer empowerment policy, because digital education both provides digital

---

[29] EU Directive 2016/1148 on security of network and information systems (NIS Directive).

[30] EU Regulation 2019/881 on ENISA (the European Union Agency for Cybersecurity) and on information and communications technology, cybersecurity certification. Repealing regulation EU N 56/2013—Cybersecurity Act.

[31] EU Commission (2021).

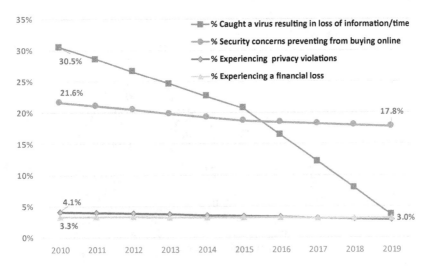

Fig. 4.1 Trend of digital problems and perception (*Source* EC Scoreboard 2020)

skills and shapes in a proper way cultural perception of both risks and opportunities.

At Fig. 4.2 below, it is showed a 2020 EU cross-country comparison which combines, on one side, the percentage of e-commerce turnover (over the overall turnover online and offline), signalling the disposition of engaging in digital transactions, and, on the other side, the percentage of individuals with at least basic digital skills.[32] Besides few outliers, it is quite evident how the two selected indicators are positively correlated and therefore countries where there is a better digital literacy have also a higher percentage of e-commerce turnovers.

As a matter of fact, digital transformation and technological innovation pushed forward the evolution of the e-commerce practices. On the other side, the deployment of innovative telecom networks, and the consequent widespread diffusion of broadband fixed and mobile connections represented a necessary enabler for the development of web-based

---

[32] In each of the following four dimensions: information, communication, problem solving and software for content creation (as measured by the number of activities carried out during the previous 3 months).

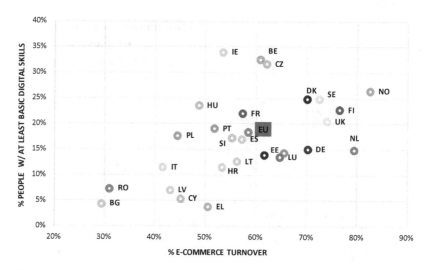

Fig. 4.2 Correlation between digital literacy and e-commerce turnover (*Source* EC Scoreboard 2020)

e-commerce. Telecommunications networks are the facility backbones for all electronic commerce activities and therefore coverage and capacity of fixed and mobile (ultra) BB network is crucial for the diffusion of e-commerce, among consumers and SMEs.[33]

All of these are constitutive elements of the fundamental multifaceted principle of access to the Internet. Since the use of internet is considered an essential element of the social and economic participation of people to the digital age, another fundamental right for concerns the Universal Access to Internet (UAI). A policy aimed to make such right effective must involve (a) the deployment of very high-capacity networks; (b) the supply of access services by internet service providers (ISP) at adequate quality and affordable prices; and (c) the ability to access and circulate contents and information, including self-generated ones, in a non-discriminatory way.

While (a) and (b) refer respectively to ultra-BB networks deployment policy,[34] and universal service regulatory obligations (USO) imposed by

---

[33] Manganelli and Nicita (2020); OECD (1999).

[34] Manganelli and Nicita (2020), Sects. 2.1 and 6.

regulators on telecom networks operator(s), (c) represents one side of the so-called "net neutrality" policy.[35]

Indeed, both in the US and in the EU, the net neutrality debate has been developed under the conceptual framework of non-discriminatory and universal access to digital services and content. Along these lines, the EU developed its position within the Open Internet Regulation (OIR)[36] by granting end-users with enforceable rights to access and distribute information, content and, services.[37] Indeed, under the OIR, Internet Service Providers must "treat all traffic equally ... without discrimination, restriction, or interference, and irrespective of the sender and receiver, the content accessed or distributed, the applications or services used or provided, or the terminal equipment used".[38] Furthermore, the regulation defines transparency obligations for Internet Service Providers, in addition to those existing for electronic communication service providers,[39] thus creating an even wider regulatory asymmetry and unlevelled playing field between telecom companies, on the one hand, and digital platforms, on the other.

Differently from universal service in the electronic communication sector, the OIR has not entailed regulatory obligations for the providers of those services whose universal access should be guaranteed, i.e., content and application providers (CAPs), but on Internet Service Providers (and/or telecom network operators). A more symmetric arrangement would have been, instead, to extend the scope and rationale of the geo-blocking regulation, by prohibiting digital services and content providers to discriminate and deny access to end-users.

---

[35] Manganelli and Nicita (2020), Sect. 8.3.

[36] EU Regulation 2015/2120 laying down measures concerning open internet access (Open Internet Regulation, OIR).

[37] Article 3(1) Open Internet Regulation (OIR).

[38] Article 3(3) OIR. Nevertheless, "reasonable" day-to-day traffic management practices are allowed as long as they are (a) transparent, (b) non-discriminatory, (c) proportionate and (d) not based on any commercial considerations but on objectively different technical quality of service requirements for specific traffic categories. Regulation also allows for the provision of specialised services, deemed as those services that need to be carried out at a specific level of quality that cannot be assured by the standard best effort delivery. See, BEREC Guidelines on the Implementation by National Regulators of European Net Neutrality Rules, BoR (16) 127.

[39] Article 4 OIR.

In the next two sections, legislation, and policies about consumer protection (Sect. 4.3) and e-privacy and data protections (Sect. 4.4) will be described and assessed both as individual rights and constitutive elements of the Digital Market Society. Those pieces of EU legislation still are the more complete set of rules so far applied to digital environment by public bodies, whereas many other aspects in the digital world are still left to "private regulation", while public rules (e.g., Data Markets Act, Data Service Act, Data Governance Act, Data Act) are under construction.

4.3   Consumer Protection: Core Values and Adaptation to Web

Over the last decades the European Union has paid a greater and greater attention to consumer issues. Indeed, it has developed a comprehensive consumer policy, under the Treaty provision setting protection of consumer as one of the Union's main objectives.[40] Furthermore, trustful, and empowered consumers are a condition for the substantial establishment of an EU-wide single market without any internal obstacles to the free movement of goods and services, which is an objective at the heart of the European project.[41]

Digital transformation has profoundly affected economies and societies, changing the ways in which consumers interact with each other and with the online intermediaries. Most of these changes are extremely positive, as mere examples: the increase of consumers' choices, augmented comparability of products and services, smarter contractual process, digitised content always available anywhere, reduction of transaction and search costs, personalised products and services. Some other changes have a potential negative impact, such as enhanced information asymmetries and inadequate disclosures, increasing misleading and unfair commercial practices, more consumer frauds, lack of cross-border enforcement and dispute resolution.[42]

---

[40] Under Article 169 TFEU.

[41] The protection of consumers is an essential part of safeguarding the EU internal market, which establishment and protection is set out as an objective in articles 26 and 114 of the TFEU.

[42] OECD (2019).

If consumer protection has been a fundamental piece of legislation for the construction and consolidation of the internal market, then it is even more decisive in the digital world, because (a) only a protected consumer is confident and can trust an online transaction; (b) there is the need to remedy an inherent consumers' lack of information about sellers, products and how the purchasing works; (c) consumer empowerment, more than in traditional market, can play a disciplining role on companies and markets.

All these elements has built a market context in which consumer protection core values should be preserved and EU cross-sectorial (horizontal) consumer legislation has represented the base for defining digital rights of internet users.[43]

First of all, the long-standing horizontal consumer protection directives fully applies to digital markets. Those directives have a twofold purpose[44]: (a) effective market fairness, by protecting the weaker party in the commercial relationships; and (b) establishment of the Internal Market through a harmonisation of national consumer protection rules. The main EU cross-sectorial consumer-oriented directives are the Directive on unfair contract terms, adopted in 1993,[45] the Directive on unfair commercial practice, adopted in 2005,[46] and the Consumer rights directive, adopted in 2011.[47]

Specifically, the Unfair Contract Terms Directive (UCTD) protects consumers against non-individually negotiated (standard) terms set by traders. This is relevant for online services and become crucial once we consider the Terms of Service (ToS) defined by platforms that may represent a private regulation and a private legal ordering (Sect. 4.1). According to the UCTD, standard contract terms must be drafted in plain intelligible language and ambiguities are to be interpreted in favour of consumers. Contract terms non-individually negotiated are unfair and, therefore, not binding on consumers if they cause a significant imbalance

---

[43] Howells et al. (2017); Howells (2020)

[44] Mateja and Micklitz (2017).

[45] Directive 93/13/EC on Unfair Terms in Consumers' Contracts.

[46] Directive 2005/29/EC, concerning unfair business-to-consumer commercial practices in the internal market. Unfair Commercial Practice Directive (UCPD).

[47] Directive 2011/83/EC on Consumers' Rights.

in the parties' rights and obligations to the detriment of the consumer.[48] The Annex define an indicative and non-exhaustive list of terms that may be regarded as unfair, illustrating the general requirement of *good faith* to which standard contract terms should abide by. Among those, it is considered unfair a contract term enabling the seller or supplier to alter the terms of the contract unilaterally without a valid reason which is specified in the contract, which limits the possibility to unilaterally amend "private regulations".

The Consumer Rights Directive (CRD) harmonises national consumer rules about certain aspects of contractual relationship, i.e., pre-contractual information requirements, formal requirements for the conclusion of contracts, detailed rules regarding the consumer's right of withdrawal. Those aspects are particularly relevant for digital markets with specific regards of distance and off-premises contracts.

The main objective of the Directive on unfair commercial practices (UCPD) is to boost consumer confidence, by enabling national enforcers to curb a broad range of unfair business practices taking place before, during and after a transaction. The Directive identifies: (a) a list of specific illicit practices[49]; (b) few general categories, i.e., misleading actions or omissions and aggressive practices[50]; and (c) a general principle under which is unfair any practice contrary to *professional diligence*.[51] A significant example for prevention of non-contractual barriers to switching regards "use of harassment, coercion and undue influence".[52] This provision prevents traders from imposing any disproportionate non-contractual barriers detrimental to consumers who wish to exercise their rights, including the right to terminate the contract or switch to another product or trader.

These directives are horizontal and are principle-based so that their provisions had a sufficiently wide scope to mostly catch the evolution of services, sales methods, and companies caused by digital transformation.

---

[48] Article 3 UCPD.

[49] Annex I UCPD.

[50] Article 6, 7, 8 UCPD.

[51] Article 5 UCPD. 'Professional diligence' means the standard of special skill and care which a trader may reasonably be expected to exercise towards consumers, commensurate with honest market practice and/or the general principle of good faith in the trader's field of activity, art 2 (h) UCPD.

[52] Article 9(d) UCPD.

Indeed, many of the current consumer rules have been flexible enough to adapt via judicial interpretation.[53] Therefore, the core horizontal consumer law directives remained a base essentially fit for purpose.[54] Of course, this base needed (and for some aspects still needs) an adaptation in order to address specific online issues, in order to maintain a protection similar to what granted to consumers in the brick-and-mortar world. "In the digital space, we need to make sure that the same rights that apply offline can be fully exercised online".[55]

Therefore, despite the flexibility of horizontal consumer legislation, policy makers have recognised the need to do more to keep up with the pace of change inherent to digital transformation, by providing consumers with well-tailored protections and with the tools enabling them to participate effectively in the Digital Market Society. Over and above judicial adaptation, EU institutions engaged in a legislative amendment process of EU consumers policy, promoted by the Communication "new Deal for Consumers".[56] This revision has been eventually enacted in 2019 by the Directive on better enforcement and modernisation of EU consumer protection (MD), which amends all three horizontal directives, i.e., UCTD, CRD, UCPD.[57] The MD's main revisions concerned:

(a) Ranking of consumer online search results: digital service providers must inform consumers, in "a concise, easily accessible and intelligible form", on the main parameters determining their ranking and relative importance.[58] Moreover, another extremely relevant provision is that traders are prohibited from "[p]roviding search results in response to a consumer's online search query without

---

[53] Pollicino (2021).

[54] European Commission (2017) Staff Working Documents: SWD (2017)169 and SWD (2017)209, respectively on the Evaluation of the Consumers' Right Directive and on the Fitness Check of the Unfair Commercial Practices and other Directives.

[55] European Commission (2021).

[56] European Commission (2018)

[57] Directive (EU) 2019/2161 as regards Better Enforcement and Modernisation of Union Consumer Protection Rules (Modernisation Directive, MD).

[58] Recitals 20 – 23 and Article 3, para. 4(b); Article 4, para. 5 MD.

clearly disclosing any paid advertisement or payment specifically for achieving higher ranking of products within the search results".[59]

(b) A new definition of marketplace, which has been updated to make it technology neutral. The Directive defines online marketplace as "a service using software, including a website or an application."[60] Furthermore, in order to increase transparency in online marketplaces, providers of online marketplaces must inform customers whether the third party is a trader or non-trader (i.e., consumer) in accordance with the self-declaration of the third party (i.e., providers do not need to verify that information). This is extremely important, since, in the case of a contract with non-traders, EU consumer protection laws do not apply.[61]

(c) Digital content and digital services provided with no monetary price, yet in implicit exchange of personal data, are included in the extended scope of the consumer rights directive. This provision aligns the definitions of digital content and digital services with their respective definitions in Directive (EU) 2019/770 Concerning Contracts for the Supply of Digital Content and Digital Services.[62] Digital content providers are now considered to be "continuous suppliers over a period of time" (as opposed to "suppliers of a single act"). As a result of this change, consumers must be granted a 14-day test period of the service and the ability to cancel the online contract within that period.[63]

(d) Personalised prices: consumers must be informed if prices offered to them are personalised on the basis of automated decision-making systems (i.e., algorithms) that profiles their behaviour and consumption patterns.[64]

---

[59] Article 3, para. 7(a) MD.

[60] Article 3, para. 1(b); Article 4, para. 1(e) MD.

[61] Article 3, para. 4(a)(ii) and Recital 28 MD.

[62] Recitals 31 – 33 and Article 4, para. 1(d) MD. As it is also the case for Directive (EU) 2019/770, which provides common rules on certain requirements concerning contracts for the supply of digital content or digital services, in particular on: (a) the conformity of digital content or a digital service with the contract, (b) remedies in the event of a lack of such conformity or a failure to supply, and the modalities for the exercise of those remedies, and (c) the modification of digital content or a digital service.

[63] Article 4, para. 11(b) and Recital 30 MD.

[64] Recital 45 M.

(e) Price Reductions: in order to prevent fake price reductions, resulting from increasing prices just before announcing price reductions, any announcement made for a price reduction must indicate the prior price of the product. The prior price of the product is the lowest price in the last 30 days before the price reduction.[65]

(f) Consumer Reviews: traders are prohibited from submitting fake consumer reviews or commissioning fake reviews or endorsements.[66] When consumer reviews are provided, traders must inform consumers if and how they ensure that the submitted reviews originate from consumers who have actually used or purchased the product.[67]

(g) Use of Bots: traders are prohibited from reselling event tickets purchased through automated means such as bot software and thus exceeding the limit imposed on the number of tickets that may be purchased.[68]

These MD measures, jointly with proposals included in the Digital services package proposal, i.e., the Digital market act and Digital service act (which are described and commented respectively in Sect. 6.3 and Sect. 7.5), provide a systemic European approach to fundamental rights of online consumers.

Notwithstanding, considering the large market and bargaining power that online platforms reached (see Sect. 5), the digital ecosystem required the extension of some "consumer-like" protection also to (more or less small) businesses, when using platforms' online intermediation services. This piece of legislation is extremely important considering the two-sided market structure (described in Sect. 2.3) which very often characterise platform economy, where business users interact (mostly) indirectly with consumers and do their own online businesses (mostly) by acquiring intermediation services from digital platforms.

[65] Article 2, para. 1 MD.

[66] Article 3, para. 7(b) MD.

[67] Article 3, para. 4(c) MD.

[68] Article 3, para. 7(b).

The relationship between platforms and businesses was addressed by the EU with the so-called Platform to business (P2B) Regulation[69] aimed to provide fairness and transparency to business users. As for its scope, the Regulation binds online intermediation and marketing services provided to business users located in the EU, at least for part of the transaction. In addition, also platforms facilitating transaction between business users and consumers are covered by the Regulation.

This piece of legislation governs the conduct of online platforms, such as software application stores, social media, e-commerce marketplaces, and search engines. The new rules mandate internal complaint-handling mechanisms to ensure ranking transparency and prohibits certain unfair practices, such as changing online terms and conditions without a justifiable reason.

As for terms and conditions (Article 3), platforms must provide contractual content that are clearly intelligible for business users and transparent as the way in which goods and services will be marketed. Changes to the terms and conditions should comply with a notice period of at least 15 days. No retroactive changes to terms and conditions are allowed. Pursuant to Article 4, if a platform provider intends to suspend or restrict access to its facility, a statement of reasons justifying the decision must be provided to the business user. In case of termination, 30 days of prior notice are required (unless the user has repeatedly violated its obligations).

As to ranking transparency (Article 5), platforms providers are mandated to make visible to the public the up-to-date parameters (e.g., specific signals deployed into algorithms, general criteria, or other adjustment methods) on the base of which rankings are formed. The actual functioning of the algorithm does not need to be disclosed (in order to safeguard innovation incentives for platforms). The reasons for the alleged significance of these parameters must be provided as well. In the spirit of disclosure, the Regulation force platforms providers to explain any possibility to actively interfere with the ranking against certain forms of remuneration by business users. If no contractual relationship between the platform and the user is in place, this should be made easily available to the public.

---

[69] Regulation (EU) 2019/1150 on promoting fairness and transparency for business users of online intermediation services (P2B Regulation).

Finally, pursuant to Article 7, platform providers must provide an exhaustive justification of any differentiated treatment between certain business users on their platform. Such an explanation must focus on the commercial and legal rationales for such unlevel treatment.

Continuous monitoring of the application of these rules is be crucial to ensure that the Regulation does not become soon outdated and that it is at pace with technological evolution. The EC is entrusted with the task to oversee this process together with Member States.[70] In this context, the EC planned to establish a broad information exchange network with association of business users, platform providers and the Observatory on the Online Platform Economy.[71]

4.4 Digital privacy: Data Protection, and Data portability

Digital and platform economy are often associated also with "data economy". The data economy involves the generation, collection, storage, processing, distribution, analysis, elaboration, delivery, and exploitation of data, all enabled by digital technologies.[72] Therefore, each policy facilitating these activities and, generally, any valorisation of data, by ensuring data aggregation, accessibility and usability, is shaping the data market regulatory framework.

When we talk about data economy and data market, we mainly talk about non-personal data, which is any set of data that do not contain any element to make it possible to identify a person. Non-personal dataset either has no personal information (such as traffic data, weather data and so on); or there is personal data included but it cannot be linked to a specific person because of anonymisation processes.

In this regard, in 2018, the EU institutions adopted a Regulation to establish a common framework for the free flow of non-personal data

---

[70] Recital 47, 49, P2B Regulation.

[71] The EU Observatory on the Online Platform Economy monitors and analyses the online platform economy, supporting the Commission in policymaking. The Observatory is made up of a group of Commission officials and a dedicated expert group of prominent independent experts, which was firstly established by a 2018 EC decision, and recently renewed in 2021 (the 2nd term of the expert group).

[72] European Data Market study (2016).

in the European Union,[73] aimed to ensure (a) free movement of non-personal data across borders: every organisation should be able to store and process data anywhere in the EU, (b) the availability of data for regulatory control: public authorities will retain access to data, even when it is located in another EU country or when it is stored or processed in the cloud, (c) easier switching between cloud service providers for professional users. The EC started facilitating self-regulation in this area, encouraging providers to develop codes of conduct regarding the conditions under which users can move data between cloud service providers and back into their own IT environments, and clarification that any security requirements that already apply to businesses storing and processing data will continue to do so when they store or process data across borders in the EU or in the cloud.

Nowadays, the distinction between personal and non-personal data is however not so clear-cut. The pervasive technological, economic, and social changes have tangibly influenced the way people use electronic communication services and equipment and, among other, have significantly influenced how our personal data are accessed, processed and used. Today, techniques such as machine learning make businesses able to make use of personal data on an unprecedented scale taking competitive advantages, for instance, by carrying out their activities on the basis of the processing output of collected data, thus acting more efficiently.

In this context, also consumers' personal data have become an essential economic asset, empowering a wide range of new and innovative business models, technologies, and transactions. Consequently, collecting data have become more and more important for businesses. Although the collection and processing of data bring various advantages, both to consumers (i.e., receiving dedicated offers, better services, etc.) and businesses (i.e., easier and faster identification of potential consumers, strategies set on the basis of the output of the data processed, etc.), several risks of illegal collection and processing arise when those activities are carried out.

Taking these aspects into consideration, only one year after publishing the Digital Single Market Strategy, the new General Data Protection

---

[73] Regulation (EU) 2018/1807 on a framework for the free flow of non-personal data in the European Union.

Regulation ('GDPR')[74] was adopted. The GDPR establishes a strong, coherent, and fully harmonised data protection framework in the EU, causing also non-EU-based companies to align with the EU's views and rules. Indeed, the scope of the GDPR can be classified as one of the most wide-ranging legislation passed by the EU, as it applies whenever personal data is processed, and imposes controls on such data also outside the EU, even for companies that have no physical presence in Europe.

GDPR represents a milestone in the achievement of a further protection of data, in comparison to the previous EU legislation, which comprised the Data Protection Directive (which became substantially out-to-date during the fast and momentous digitalisation) and the "ePrivacy" Directive, which is still in force and applicable.

To sum up, the GDPR aims to govern the processing of personal data (that is "any information relating to an identified or identifiable natural person, or a data subject") in order to ensure that personal data can only be gathered under strict conditions and for legitimate purposes. In particular, personal data must be: (a) processed lawfully, fairly and in a transparent manner; (b) collected for specified, explicit and legitimate purposes; (c) adequate, relevant and limited to what is necessary in relation to the purposes for which they are processed; (d) accurate and, where necessary, kept up to date; (e) kept in a form which permits identification of the person to whom the information is related for no longer than it is necessary; (f) processed in a manner that ensures appropriate security and protection, e.g., against unauthorised or unlawful processing, accidental loss, or destruction or damage.

An innovative right enshrined in the GDPR is one of data portability. That's a breakthrough in the realm of EU personal data protection law. In fact, this innovation can be read as the first bold complement to the Digital Single Market Strategy launched by the European Commission in 2015.[75] Moreover, such new regime represents a corner-stone of the European data common space, since a substantial part of the data flowing throughout the DSM is composed of personal data, according

---

[74] Regulation (EU) 2016/6791 on the protection of natural persons with regard to the processing of personal data and on the free movement of such data and repealing Directive 95/46/EC (General Data Protection Regulation, GDPR). The regulation was adopted in May 2016 and became applicable as of May 2018.

[75] European Commission (2015).

to the broad definition set forth in the GDPR.[76] By introducing this legislative instrument, the EU sought to empower individuals by granting them more control over their personal data.[77] Leaving aside the access-to-account rule under the Revised Payment Services Directive (PSD2),[78] no attempt to enact a similar regulatory initiative has been pursued before.[79]

On a more technical note, the objective scope of portability is limited to personal data that data subject has provided to a data controller.[80] Data portability encompasses three different and complementary rights: (a) the right to receive data provided by data subject; (b) the right to move those data to another controller; and (c) the right to have the personal data transferred directly from one controller to another, where technically feasible. With (c), it becomes very clear that the ultimate goal behind the right to data portability is delivering interconnection and interoperability of all digital services within the DSM. Clearly, data controllers are strictly forbidden from hindering the exercise of those rights by individuals.[81]

Data portability right can be read, as it will be detailed in Sect. 6, as a necessary (yet not sufficient) complement to a policy aimed at counterbalancing the asymmetric interaction between platform and users, by enabling switching of service providers. Indeed, by affirming individuals' control over their personal data, data portability is expected to tackle personal data lock-in problems as well as to encourage competition between companies.[82] The rationale for the data portability right fits better within a competition policy framework than it does on traditional data protection systems hinged on Article 8 of the EU Charter of Fundamental Rights.

---

[76] GDPR, Article 4.

[77] Article 29 Data Protection Working Party (2017), 2; GDPR, Recital 68. See also Colangelo and Maggiolino (2019).

[78] Directive (EU) 2015/2366 which replaced the Payment Services Directive (PSD), Directive 2007/64/EC.

[79] Custers and Ursic (2016).

[80] A data controller is "any natural or legal person, public authority, agency or other body which, alone or jointly with others, determines the purposes and means of the processing of personal data" GDPR, Article 20.

[81] GDPR, Article 20.

[82] Article 29 Data Protection Working Party (2017), 4. See also European Commission (2018).

End-users empowerment by means of individual control over personal data has the potential to unlock competition within data-driven markets.[83] Thus, the main goal underpinning data portability is the promotion of competition among data-enabled service providers, also by establishing an "early form" of personal data subjects' default ownership. Even if, property would entail the right to exclude anyone, which is currently not provided by the right to data portability under the GDPR. Similarly, the right to erasure (so called 'right to be forgotten') under the GDPR (Article 17) cannot be considered a full proprietary tool, due to its extremely limited (and highly contested) applicability.[84]

As it stands, the right to personal data portability is likely to prove problematic with regards to its implementation. In fact, Article 20(1) of the GDPR does not provide detailed guidance on how to ensure data portability among undertakings. It merely states a general requirement for the format of transmitted data, which need to be "structured, commonly used and machine readable". That is to say, file formats structured in such a way that software applications can easily identify, recognise and extract specific data from them.[85] Further, any attempt to mandate the adoption of interoperable standards is excluded as Recital 68 of GDPR does not go beyond a simple "encouragement". Such lack of any binding provision or detailed guideline covering the implementation of data portability is likely to raise serious concerns on effectiveness and legal certainty. Interoperability and portability need to be made effective, otherwise they will remain a dead letter.

Next to the recent GDPR rules, the EU has been regulating privacy in the electronic communications sector (so called e-privacy) since the 2002. The e-privacy directive[86] aimed to ensure that all communications over electronic communications networks maintain a high level of data protection and privacy with regard of confidentiality of communications,

---

[83] Costa-Cabral and Lynskey (2017).

[84] On this point, see Graef, Husovec, Purtova (2018). Instead, for a view supporting a full proprietary setting, see De Hert, Papakonstantinou, Malgieri, Baslay, and Sanchez (2018).

[85] Directive 2013/37/EU of the European Parliament and of the Council of 26 June 2013 amending Directive 2003/98/EC on the re-use of public sector information [2013] OJ L175, Recital 21.

[86] Directive 2002/58/EC concerning the processing of personal data and protection of privacy in the electronic communications sector.

traffic data, location data, directory of subscribers and unsolicited calls. In January 2017 the European Commission adopted a proposal for a Regulation on Privacy and Electronic Communications to replace the ePrivacy Directive and adapting the sector-specific legislation to GDPR.[87] Key points of the proposal are: (a) enhancing the protection of users applying privacy rules to new players providing electronic communications services, i.e., number-independent interpersonal communication services (e.g., WhatsApp, Facebook Messenger and Skype); (b) ensuring a level plying filed by guaranteeing privacy for all communications content and metadata, e.g. time of a call and location, which must be kept in an anonymous form or deleted if users did not give their consent; (c) simplification and streamlining of rules on cookies; (d) protection against unsolicited electronic communications and information society services (spam), e.g., by default or using a do-not-call list; (e) marketing callers will need to be identifiable; (f) allocating the enforcement of the confidentiality rules to data protection authorities, already in charge of the rules under the General Data Protection Regulation. Indeed, especially considering a systemic dimension, the e-privacy rules must be coherent with the general GDPR, first of all with regards to explicit consent. Also because, e-privacy regulation of the digital identity is a pre-requisite also for data portability.

References

Akerlof, G., & Schiller, R. (2009). *Animal spirits. How human psychology drives the economy, and why it matters for global capitalism.* Princeton University Press, p. 21.

Allcott, H., & Sunstein, C. (2015). Regulating internalities. *Journal of Policy Analysis and Management, 34*(3), 698.

Barlow, J. P. (1996). A declaration of the independence of cyberspace, 8 February 1996.

Belli, L., & Venturini, J. (2016). Private ordering and the rise of terms of service as cyber regulation. *Internet Policy Review, 5*(4).

BEREC. (2013). *Report on the NRAs' regulatory capacity.*

BEREC. (2016). Guidelines on the Implementation by National Regulators of European Net Neutrality Rules, BoR (16) 127.

---

[87] European Commission (2017) Proposal for a Regulation on Privacy and Electronic Communications. COM (2017) 10 final.

Cafaggi, F. (2004). Le rôle des acteurs privés dans les processus de régulation: Participation, autorégulation et régulation privée. Revue Française d'Administration Publique 2004/1 (no109).

Colangelo, G., & Maggiolino, M. (2019). From fragile to smart consumers: Shifting paradigm for the digital era. *Computer Law & Security Review, 35*(2), 173–181.

Costa-Cabral, F., & Lynskey, O. (2017). Family ties: The intersection between data protection and competition in EU law. *Common Market Law Review, 54*(1), 11–50.

Custers, B., & Ursic, H. (2016). Big data and data reuse: A taxonomy of data reuse for balancing big data benefits and personal data protection. *International Data Privacy Law, 6*(1), 4–15.

De Hert, P., Papakonstantinou, V., Malgieri, G., Baslay, L., & Sanchez, I. (2018). The right to data portability in the GDPR: Towards user-centric interoperability of digital services. *Computer Law and Security Review 193.*

De Streel, A., & Ledger, M. (2020). *New ways of oversight for the digital economy.* CERRE Issue Paper.

Elkin-Koren, N. (1997). *Copyright policy and the limits of freedom of contract.* Berkeley Tech. L.J. 93.

European Commission. (2015). *A digital single market strategy for Europe.* COM 2015/0192/final.

European Commission. (2017). Proposal for a *Regulation concerning the respect of private life and the protection of personal data in the Electronic Communications, and repealing Directive 2002/58 (Regulation on Privacy and Electronic Communications).* COM/2017/10 final.

European Commission. (2018). *Communication: A new deal for consumers.* COM/2018/0183 final.

European Commission. (2021). *Digital Compass 2030 – The European way for the Digital Decade.* COM/2021/218 final.

European Commission. (2022). *European declaration on digital rights and principles for the digital decade.*

European Data Market study, SMART 2013/0063, IDC, 2016.

Goldsmith, J., & Wu, T. (2006). *Who controls the internet?* Oxford University Press.

Graef, I., Husovec, M., & Purtova, N. (2018). Data portability and data control: Lessons for an emerging concept in EU law. *German Law Journal, 19*(6), 1359–1398.

Hobbes, T. (1651). *Leviathan or the matter, form and power of a commonwealth ecclesiasticall and civil.*

Howells, G. (2020). Protecting consumer protection values in the fourth industrial revolution. *Journal of Consumer Policy, 43*, 145–175.

Howells, G. Twigg-Flesner, C., & Willett, C. (2017). Product liability and digital products. In T. –E. Synodinou, P. Jogleux, C. Markou, & T. Prastitou (Eds.), *EU Internet Law* (pp. 183–195). Springer International Publishing.

Kaye, D. (2018). *Report of the special rapporteur on the promotion and protection of the right to freedom of opinion and expression*. U.N. Doc. A/HRC/38/35

Kelsen, H. (1960). 2d ed. Pure *Theory of Law*. The Reine Rechtslehre.

Kelsen, H., & Paulson, S. (1982). The concept of the legal order. *The American Journal of Jurisprudence, 27*(1), 64–84.

Lessig, L. (2000). *Code is law. On liberty in cyberspace*. Harvard Magazine 1.1.00.

Lessig, L. (2006). *Code 2.0*. On liberty in cyberspace. Basic Books.

Locke, J. (1689). *Two treatises of* government - *Second Treatise*.

MacCormick, N. (1999). *Questioning sovereignty*. Oxford University Press.

Manganelli, A., & Nicita, A. (2020). *The governance of telecom markets*. Palgrave Macmillan.

Mateja, D., & Micklitz, H. W. (2017). *Internationalization of consumer law*. Springer.

OECD. (1999). The economic and social impact of electronic commerce: Preliminary findings and research agenda. OECD Publishing.

OECD. (2009). *Better regulation in Europe: An assessment of regulatory capacity in 15 member states of the European Union*.

OECD. (2019). *Digital consumers challenge*. OECD Publishing.

Pollicino, O. (2021). *Judicial protection of fundamental rights on the internet. A road towards digital constitutionalism?* Hart Publishing.

Romano, S. (2017). *The legal order*. Edited and translated by Croce, M.

Simon, H. (1955). A Behavioural Model of Rational Choice. *Quarterly Journal of Economics, 69*(1), 99.

Smith, A. (1759). *Theory of moral sentiments*.

Smith, A. (1776). *An inquiry into the nature and causes of the wealth of nations*. Methuen & Co (Book IV, chapter 8, 49).

Srnicek, N. (2016). *Platform capitalism*. Wiley.

Srnicek, N. (2017). *We need to nationalise Google, Facebook and Amazon. Here's why*. theguardian.com, 30 August 2017.

Thaler, R. (1985). Mental accounting and consumer choice. *Marketing Science, 4*(3), 199–214.

Wu, T. (2009). When code isn't law. *Virgina Law Review 679* (89).

Zumbansen, P. (2013). Transnational private regulatory governance ambiguities of public authority and private power. *Law and Contemporary Problems*, vol. 76.

PART II

Regulating Big Techs' Impact on Market and Society

CHAPTER 5

Understanding Market Power in the Digital Market Society

Abstract The main digital players are today (few) large global platforms, with a high degree of vertical and horizontal integration in many segments of the digital ecosystem. According to many scholars, due to economies of scale and scope, indirect and direct network externalities and consumers behavioural biases, in most cases digital markets are subject to 'tipping'. This implies a winner-takes-it-all scenario once the leading company, often called 'gatekeeper', reaches a certain scale. Other scholars, however, contend that dominance over distinct relevant markets, rather than 'tipping', should continue to provide the criteria to assess platforms' market power. The observed platforms dynamics are however based on new economic transactions where data is implicitly exchanged for free services, beyond specific relevant markets. Furthermore, information revealed to platforms and 'appropriated' by them, is not perfectly observable by everyone, but (*de facto*) internalised and exclusively exploited. Big platforms, as global gatekeepers, are not just competing for the market. They envisage a new institutional ordering in which they actually compete, through 'envelopment' strategies, to 'become' the market.

Keywords Big Techs' economics · Market and economic power · Data and algorithms · Information

© The Author(s), under exclusive license to Springer Nature
Switzerland AG 2022
A. Manganelli and A. Nicita, *Regulating Digital Markets*,
Palgrave Studies in Institutions, Economics and Law,
https://doi.org/10.1007/978-3-030-89388-0_5

107

5.1   Global Digital Platforms: From Competitive Advantage to Market 'Tipping'

Online platforms are multisided intermediaries that operate, with different business models, in several industries (e.g., search engines, social media and creative content outlets, application distribution platforms, communications services, payment systems, and platforms for the collaborative economy) (see Sects. 5.2 and 5.3).

Looking at companies' global ranking for market capitalisation, as described in Sect. 1.2, the relevance of digital platforms in today's economy is blatant: in 2019, 7 out of the top 10 companies are digital platforms and there are 4 platforms at the top 4 positions. The USA-based platforms in the top 10 ranking, i.e., Amazon, Facebook, Google, Apple, Microsoft (to which often is added Netflix) are also known as the "Big Techs". Indeed, Big Techs are those digital platforms with global dimension and a paramount scale, having very high market shares in their own market segment(s), as described in the Table 5.1, where relative share of markets and the related ranking position can be observed.

Table 5.1   Big Techs' market share in respective segments

	Google		amazon		Apple		facebook		Microsoft		NETFLIX	
	Share	Rank	Share	Rank	Share	Rank	Share	Rank	Share	Rank	Share	Rank
Cloud (IaaS) Revenues, 2018	4%	4	48%	1					16%	2		
Vocal assistance Smart speaker number, 2019	31%	2	32%	1	6%	6						
Device (mobile) Revenue, 2018					50%	1						
Operating systems (desktop) Pages viewed, Nov-2018/Oct-2019	1%	5			14%	2			77%	1		
Operating systems (mobile) Pages viewed, Nov-2018/Oct-2019	75%	1			23%	2			0,2%	5		
Browser Pages viewed, Nov-2018/Ott-2019	64%	1			15%	2			5%	4		
Online advertising Revenues, 2018	32%	1	3%	4			19%	2	2%	7		
E-commerce Revenues			n.a.[*]	1								
App store (mobile) Revenues (Android and iOS), Jun-2019	38%	2			62%	1						
Audio-visual content (VoD) Revenues, 2018	n.a	n.a			n.a						51%	1

Source AGCOM (2019) Report on online platforms

As mentioned, for digital platforms, which are two-sided markets, free service on one side of the platform are also crucial. The relative ranking and "market share" are reported in the Table 5.2.

This concentration outcome of course depends on classical market dynamics, i.e., R&D, innovation, marketing, customer care, advertising and so on, but also on some specific economic characteristics of digital platforms, as those that we outlined in previous chapters.

In 2018, the cash-flow of the leading five platforms touched on 160 billion euros. This has allowed these global operators to invest, in only one year, more than 50 billion euros. This is an enormous amount of investments for technologies and network infrastructures, which have been completely self-financed (while for example in the telecom sector there is need of substantial debt capitals). As shown in the Fig. 5.1 below, on average in 2018 only 37% of platforms' cash-flow has been absorbed in assets investments against telecoms where asset investments sum up 145% of their cash-flow.

This is not because Big tech invests less than Telcos, on the contrary, on average they invest much more (globally) yet also have much higher revenue and profitability.

From a market concentration viewpoint, these characteristics are very relevant, firstly because Big techs have paramount revenues, profits and investment capacity (they have very 'deep pockets') which are extremely difficult for new entrants to match; secondly, the financial liquidity available to digital platforms has allowed them to a merger and acquisition strategy of potential competitors or complementors (supplier of complement service/products, which are anyway potential competitors in a digital conglomerates context). This strategy was evocatively defined as 'killer acquisitions'[1] and ultimately led the FTC to start, in 2021, a retrospective investigation over the Facebook-WhatsApp merger (see Box 5.1).

Box 5.1 Killer Acquisitions

The "killer acquisition" kind of structural market strategy is not new, but practised to a certain extent in some other industry with

---

[1] OECD (2020) and Tirole (2020).

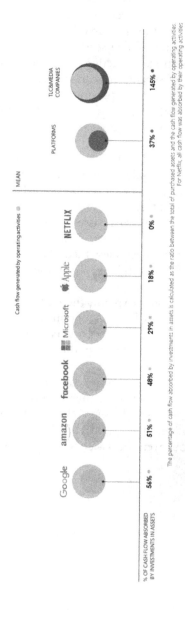

Fig. 5.1 Big Techs' cash flow (%) absorbed by investments in assets (*Source* AGCOM [2019])

Table 5.2 Big Techs' market share in the "free" side of the market

	Google		facebook	
	Share	Rank	Share	Rank
Q Search Minutes spent in a month in Europe (EU5), Oct-18/Sept-19	88%	1		
Social network Minutes spent in a month in Europe (EU5), Oct-18/Sept-19			76%	1
Instant messaging Minutes spent in a month in Europe (EU5), Oct-18/Sept-19	1%	4	95%	1
Email Pages viewed in a month in Europe (EU5), Oct-18/Sept-19	53%	1		
Maps Minutes spent in a month in Europe (EU5), Oct-18/Sept-19	91%	1		
App store (mobile) Global number of downloads, 2018	72%	1		

Source AGCOM (2019)

very concentred market shares, e.g., the ICT and pharmaceutical industry. For example, empirical findings from the pharmaceutical industry show that 6% of the acquisitions considered were followed by the stop of new product development activities previously pursued by the target.[2] There is no yet a similar direct empirical evidence on digital markets, nevertheless the transposition of this narrative to Big Techs has been motivated by the idea that tech giants intentionally acquire promising start-up companies or potential competitors to "hold the fort" and "kill" future competition. Namely, the acquisition of (potential) competitors or providers of complementary services in neighbouring markets is feared to

[2] Cunningham et al. (2021).

result in marginalisation of rivals (the "killer acquisition" concern) and higher barriers to entry (the "digital conglomerate" concern). Indeed, Big Techs have intensively engaged in mergers and acquisitions (M&A) activity. Between 2009 and 2020, GAFA engaged in more than 400 M&A transactions.[3] Most of these were either innovative start-ups or new entrants. Admittedly, there are several reasons justifying new acquisitions by large platform-based companies. First, Big Techs might be interests in specific assets held by the target company (intellectual property, users, human resources, know-how, etc.).[4] Second, as platforms are increasingly competing for attracting the attention of users on their own platforms, acquisition of new service providers allows them to strengthen their own ecosystem, also from a conglomerate perspective.[5] Third, and more interestingly, it has been argued that acquisition could be aimed at restricting potential competition and ultimately entrenching the market power of the platform.[6] Since network effects play a prominent role for platform-based companies, a new firm which is likely to build up a substantial user base can represent a competitive threat for Big Techs even in the absence of effective product overlap at the moment of the acquisition. Despite such serious competitive concerns, very few of the mergers carried out by GAFAM were investigated by competition agencies or successfully challenged by private plaintiffs and state attorneys general in the EU and US. This is so because turnover is used as the main proxy for several merger control regimes throughout the world, including the EU. While the threshold differs according to each jurisdiction, all such tests provide to take into account the turnover of one or both of the transaction parties in a certain jurisdiction or geographical area. Against this backdrop, several high-profile M&A operations dealing with digital markets have escaped authorities review. This is because

[3] Gautier and Lamesch (2020) and O. Latham et al. (2020).

[4] Gautier and Lamesch (2020).

[5] Prat and Valletti (2021).

[6] Crémer et al. (2019).

the relevant turnover thresholds were not met despite the targets being bought for large amounts of money. As many digital start-ups use to provide their services free of charge in the first stages of development, they generate low revenues while still retaining a substantial economic value in terms of data sets and potentially large user base. Good examples were the $1 billion acquisition in 2012 of **Instagram by Facebook** or the acquisition in 2013 of the Israeli mapping services provider **Waze by Google** for $1.3 billion.[7] Similarly, the $19 billion acquisition of **WhatsApp** (a company with a turnover of around ten million dollars) **by Facebook** was reviewed by the EC only based on a specific pre-notification referral request by Facebook in order to benefit from the one-stop-shop review provided by Article 4(5) of the EU Merger Regulation (EUMR). All these transactions did not involve sufficient turnover to have an EU dimension pursuant to the EUMR. As a response to the frustration generated by this enforcement gap in merger control, new proposals have surfaced to complement the EU turnover thresholds by a test considering the value of the transaction at stake. Merger control is at the forefront of antitrust early-stage interventions in markets prone to "tipping" due to network effects resulting in "winner takes all" effects due to its ex-ante nature. Thus, it should not come as a surprise that an increasing number of proposals aimed at overhauling European competition law focus heavily on merger control.[8] Germany, for instance, has already introduced a new jurisdictional €400 million threshold based on the value of the transaction rather than the turnover of target companies. An additional solution emerged so far relies on the "share of supply" criterion already enacted in Portugal, Spain, and UK under which a merger must be notified if the market share of the resulting entity is above a certain threshold. Also, it is worth considering

---

[7] Today, Instagram, numbering almost 1 billion users, is the second social network in the world, after Facebook, and the sixth if we include also message service providers (WhatsApp, WeChat and Messenger) and social media (YouTube).

[8] Motta and Peitz (2021) and Gautier and Lamesch (2020).

the proposal to oblige largest tech companies with a special status to notify all their acquisitions so as to allow authorities to investigate their competitive impact in due advance.[9] This last proposal has been included in the Digital Market Act, as an obbligation for gatekeeper to notify to the EC about any intended concentration (within the meaning of article 3 of the EU merger regulation, 139/2004) involving any service provider in the digital sector (see Sect. 6.3). Finally, on a more substantive note, it is gaining momentum on both sides of the Atlantic the proposal to shift from antitrust authorities to the firms involved in horizontal mergers the burden of proving that the net competitive impact of the transaction is positive.[10]

As for revenues, Big Techs global income was 692 billion euros in 2018: a 35% increase compared to 2017. The top income was reported by Apple (225 billion euros, +11%), followed by Amazon (107 billion, +25%) and Google (116 billion, +18%), while the average revenue of all six platforms was 115 billion euros.

Big Techs, however, have very different features: they perform different activities and are active in different market segments of the digital market society; they also have different business models, investments strategy, level of markets' integration, differentiated approaches regarding interoperability, openness and standardisation. One of the main distinctions is the general business model and the associated revenues source. In this regard:

a. Netflix, Microsoft and Apple's incomes are based on selling services and products to end-users. Apple mainly sells ICT fixed and mobile devices; Netflix audio visual media contents; and Microsoft sells software, ICT devices and cloud services to users, but also has a secondary, much smaller, source of revenues from online advertising.
b. Facebook and Google revenues come primarily from advertisements or other business services. However, while for Facebook ads

[9] Furman et al. (2019).
[10] Motta and Peitz (2021).

revenues amount at about 95%, Google has 15% of its revenues from customer' service (mainly cloud services).

c. Amazon has a more hybrid business model, differentiating in a substantive manner its source of revenues, even if revenues from customers are predominant. For example, Amazon's e-commerce activity is divided into marketplace activity (matchmaking sellers and buyers) and direct online retailing, which is predominant (53% of its overall revenues against 18%) (Fig. 5.2).

As mentioned, the matchmaking activities, especially regarding advertising, is very often associated to free services on the users' side of the market. That's why there is no or little revenues from end-users in companies like Facebook and Google, although the former has 1.7 billion users worldwide (and 300 million in EU) for its social network and instant messaging services, and the latter has roughly 1.7 billion people using its search engine services on a daily basis, with an average of 7 billion searches per day. The stream of profits come from advertising activities targeting the users' audience.

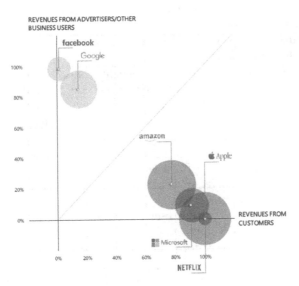

Fig. 5.2 Source of revenues for the Big Tech (*Source* AGCOM 2019)

Furthermore, Big Techs can enjoy a drastically increasing return to scale and significant economies of scope. As a matter of fact, global digital giants aim to expand more and more the scale and also the scope of their activities: a market strategy named "platform envelopment". Not all platforms have the same approach, ranging from 'specialization', through 'integration' to 'platform envelopment' (Table 5.3). The 'platform envelopment' strategy is a continuous expansion of services, supplied in distinct markets, made interoperable for the same user base combining functionalities of the origin and target markets.[11] This is the approach adopted mainly by Amazon and Google, and with a lower intensity by Microsoft and Apple. However, also Facebook providing extensive social network services, naturally envelope and embed all kind of social interactions made of 'self-generated' or self-reproduced services and content, e.g., audiovisual content, e-commerce, information content. This is indeed relevant as the main effect of the envelopment takes place on the users' side.

In this situation, platforms can leverage shared user relationships and market power on its user base by offering bundled products, therefore substantially increasing the (opportunity) cost of (a) switching to a competitor or (b) using more than one platform at the same time (*multihoming*). Moreover, platform envelopment strategies are aimed also to enlarge the information and data collected by platforms and increase their services' quality and productive efficiency by cross-checking information related to different context.

Furthermore, digital platforms can benefit from direct network externalities (i.e., economies of scale on the demand side) and indirect network externalities (cross-side network effects).[12] Direct network externalities implies that the utility for a user to use the services of a platform increases in the number of other users (relevant to him) in that platform, thus implying that a user would have to incur in a high cost to abandon a platform (switching costs) with a large number of (relevant) users. In addition, the economic value of the platform grows in relation to the expansion of its users' base.

An increase of the platform's user base would most likely result in an increase in each user's willingness to pay. However, this does not necessarily imply a price increase for joining the platform. Indeed, even when

---

[11] Eisenmann et al. (2011).

[12] Shy (2001).

Table 5.3 Scope economics and platform envelopment strategy

Industry chain stage		NETFLIX	facebook	Apple	Microsoft	Google	amazon
INFRASTRUCTURES	Cloud and Data centre				Azure	Google Cloud	AWS
ENABLING TECHNOLOGY	Device						fire
	Software (OS, Browser etc)			iOS	Windows	android	Fire OS
ONLINE SERVICES	Online advertising						
	e-commerce						amazon
	Audio-visual content	N					
	Other services						
	Communication services						

Increasing Supply variety

a platform has a significative power in some markets, it could forego increasing prices (or keep its zero-price strategy) in order to further expand its user base. This dynamic is even more clear considering the *cross-side network effects*, occurring when the utility for a member of a group of a two-sided platform increases in the number of users on the other side of that platform. As also described in Sect. 5.3, in many cases, to gain the highest number of users, matchmakers can introduce, and constantly maintain, a zero-price strategy on one side, regardless of its market power, so to increase revenues from the associated side.

Therefore, increasing returns to scale, economies of scope, indirect and direct network externalities tend to determine an increase in the level of concentration in digital markets, which in most cases are subject to a phenomenon known as 'tipping': once a platform reaches a critical mass (tipping-point), the platforms' increase in scale becomes self-sustaining because of the network effects and the users' cost-opportunity of exit, which push towards a continuous expansion of the user network, potentially up to a situation in which a single operator remains in the market, as a monopolist. From here come the expression 'winner-take-all'[13], as, at the same time, while the platform costs tend to increase constantly in the number of users, revenues increase exponentially.

Economies of scale, platform envelopments and, above all, network effects can therefore become insurmountable obstacles to actual and potential competitors, which must be able to overcome the existing 'critical mass' in order to establish and compete sustainably in the affected markets. That is not so easy, and the collective coordination costs for users to jointly move in order to decrease their unilateral cost-opportunity are not that small (only another digital platform, having users' switching as a public mission or business objective, could be able to decrease coordination costs enough to make such a collective switching choice possible and potentially convenient for users).

The evolution of big digital platforms may shed some lights on the nature of big tech's economic power. The timeline of search engines' market share evolution[14] is a very good example to show both the existence of a critical mass (approximately 40% of users), and the competitive dynamics of the markets in which really the winner takes all (Fig. 5.3).

---

[13] T. Eisenmann (2006).

[14] US market estimation from various sources—Sew, Net Applications, StatCounter.

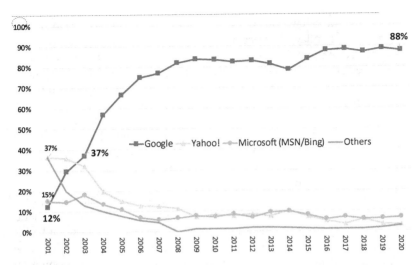

Fig. 5.3 Evolution of search engine market shares (*Source* Elaboration on Agcom [2019])

Nevertheless, this very same graph also narrates the Schumpeterian concept of 'creative destruction'. According to Schumpeter's theory, competition is fostering innovation, in order to get some monopoly's rent, until the next innovation is introduced in the market, either by the monopolist itself, in order to 'hold the fort', or by competitors, in order to besiege it. In other words, monopoly generates competition through imitative processes, but the competition generates innovations designed to maintain non-enduring monopolies. Therefore, from a Schumpeterian view, the monopoly-competition cycle is diachronic and self-disciplined.[15] This theory applied to the digital world may give hints of the inherent fragility of Big Techs' market positions. Indeed, at the beginning of 2000, Yahoo! was world leader in the search engines market, until Google overtook it. Since then, Yahoo!'s market shares have constantly and sharply decreased and currently it is a marginal player. From this viewpoint, all Big Techs' days are numbered (although nobody knows how many they are). So, even Google may be overtaken by a new competitor in a not so faraway future.

[15] Schumpeter (1934).

In a 2015 interview, Tim Berners-Lee, the "inventor" of the Web, has recognised that today *Facebook* and *Google* have characteristics of dominance, but added that so was the case of *Netscape* and *Microsoft* years ago. Berners-Lee stated: "While we were fighting against the dominant position of Mountain View, Facebook and social engineering popped-up. The history of the web is an history of periodic monopolisation and monopoly alternation, but the truth is that the wind may suddenly change, and the emphasis shifts elsewhere: while we are focused on the alleged 'enemy' of the moment, new inventions come along. On the Net, there is a lot more supply than what it seems: there are big companies, but also small ones that do not profile their users".

That is to say that, as in a Schumpeterian market cycle, it is just a matter of time for competition to appear. According to this argument, "external" interventions, including antitrust investigations, would ultimately just hinder this cycle, harming innovation and, ultimately, social welfare. The same argument goes on by stressing that economies of scale, scope and direct network effects are however quite common in all network industries (e.g., telecoms, energy, water industries, and so on), and cross-side network effects are common in all two-sided platforms, also in traditional ones (e.g., newspapers, credit cards, and so on). Within this narrative, the final argument rely on the consideration that most of these market situations, when becoming abusive, could be tackled by competition law enforcement, as it actually happened (see Sect. 1.2).

In addition, some economists are of the opinion that the concept of 'tipping' and 'winner takes all', which are indeed relevant in traditional network industries, are not applicable to digital platforms because of negligible exit and direct switching costs[16] borne by users to change platforms. Moreover, it has been argued that large digital platforms that directly deal with consumers, such as GAFA, cannot possibly be "winner-take-all" firms, because these platforms must either compete on the merits or otherwise rely on exclusionary practices to attain or maintain dominance (maintaining for competition law the task of disciplining

---

[16] We must discern between, on one side, direct switching costs, being actual monetary cost to switch provider, e.g., a penalty for early termination of service provision contract, and, on the other side, indirect switching costs, which are very often opportunity costs, that is a non-monetary cost, a profit or benefit loss, like the ones related to changing affiliation from a network where most of our counterparts are.

platforms competitive conducts).[17] In this sense, in digital markets "competition is a click away".[18] This would even be more true if one thinks that using a platform does not prevent users to use another competing platform (multihoming)—for example, searching both on Google and Bing, or joining and interacting in two different social networks. Thus, also dividing overall attention among competing providers and thus also giving incentive to advertisers or anyway the platforms' other group/side to perform multihoming and finally change provider.[19]

The above Schumpeterian view has led to a "laissez-faire" approach in early days of the expansion of the digital economy, and a "wait and see" approach has characterised initial attitude of antitrust authorities around the world towards digital platforms. This approach shared much of the Chicago School theories for a conservative antitrust approach.[20] As for platforms monopolisation, a conduct forbidden under section 2 of the Sherman Act in the US, the Chicago standard outlined that exclusion is part of the success of efficient incumbent and that in order for exclusionary conducts to be deemed anticompetitive under antitrust law, the plaintiff should provide evidence of "inefficient exclusion", i.e. the direct impact of conduct towards more efficient competitors. In turn, this theory has largely neglected above-marginal-cost predation strategies and set a very challenging standard of evidence on plaintiffs.

The traditional *Chicago Approach* has been under discussion in recent years by prominent scholars,[21] who led a new movement, named *neo-Brandeisian*. One of the main arguments pointed by neo-Brandeisian again revolves around the Yahoo!-Google battle. Should the neo-Schumpeterian argument be right, why we observe a clear difference in the market share reached by Google today, compared to what Yahoo! had in 2001? In other words, why Yahoo! was not subject to tipping? And furthermore, why the period in which Yahoo! managed to lead the market was much shorter? And if all the digital platforms' economics are not

---

[17] See Hovenkamp H. (2021). See also Evans and Schmalensee (2016).

[18] Larry Page declared on 21 September 2011 before the US Senate Judiciary Committee.

[19] Multihoming behaviour would also show that attention is often divided among different platforms which could, at the same time, benefit from users' data and from the network effects.

[20] Posner (2001) and Bork (1978).

[21] Baker (2019), Khan (2016), Khan (2018) and Wu (2018).

something completely new, why competition law enforcement and merger regulation have not proved to be completely effective in tackling and, above all, preventing conducts detrimental for market and consumers?

According to the neo-Brandeisian scholars, we are now inside an ecosystem that has surpassed the Schumpeterian monopoly-competition threshold, pervasively transforming the Schumpeterian dynamics of innovation and imitation. For example, the gap between Google and any other search engine is today deemed to be too large and impossible to bridge. At the same time multihoming is always less popular and costly, and lack of interoperability measures do not allow potential competitor to have immediate access to users of the incumbent platform.

The neo-Brandeisian approach emphasises that the current digital ecosystem entered into an era where competition, always possible, becomes constrained and constrained, residual, and segmented. As, we will see in the next section most of these reasons has to do with data: Big Tech's Big data.

5.2   Data and Algorithmic Profiling: The Source of Economic Power

One of the fundamental elements of platforms' power are digital data, which—as mentioned in Sect. 5.3—is indeed an economic good, and the information that algorithms can provide by analysing this data.

Due to the massive number of users, and to the enormous time spent and number of online actions made, platforms collect an incredibly high amount of users' data. This allows platforms' algorithms to profile individual demand for services and products for all and each user, in terms of preferences, needs, and willingness to pay. Platforms rely on profiling to monetise data by either using information directly, as retailers for online trade, or indirectly, as recipients of targeted personalised advertising. Moreover, data allows algorithms to gradually improve themselves, as new data is analysed and improve estimations on users' preferences and thus the quality of profiling.

This process allows platforms to increase their matching capacity and thus increase demand on both sides of the platform: on the users' side, by increasing service productive efficiency and quality (i.e., services or products that are better suited to users' preferences and needs), on the other group side (e.g., advertisers), by increasing the number or attention of users to whom ads is addressed. All this produces incentives for platforms to collect more and more data by adopting 'zero price' business models and to expand scale and scope of their activities.

Indeed, in the digital ecosystem we can access a multitude of service for free, spending on them a lot of time and attention, thus providing a lot of data and information. The implicit exchange of free services for our data, time and attention is an actual economic transaction, although it is a non-monetary one.

To support this statement, it seems helpful to refer to an econometric study, carried in 2018[22] on a dataset comprising more than one million applications on Google Play. This study shows how applications' price is inversely correlated with the number of permissions required and thus with the number of consents on individual data. In addition, the study highlights that the most frequently downloaded Apps require more permissions related to individual data. The Apps downloads trend detects a "long tail" phenomenon, where about 50% of all the Apps are downloaded less than 100 times and about 2% more than 100,000 times. Useless to say that only 6 Apps are installed more than 1 billion times: Facebook, Google Gmail, YouTube, Google Maps, Google Search and Google Play Services.

In this context of implicit transactions and zero-price services, the evaluation of consumer welfare is not trivial. In the classical notion of social welfare, consumers freedom of choice and potential competition plays crucial roles as drivers for market growth and innovation.

In theory, by means of massive and sophisticated user profiling, platforms can understand the willingness to pay of each user for each good or service and implement a *perfect* (first degree) *price discrimination*—i.e., charging a price for each consumer and for each unit of product equal to the maximum price that consumer would pay, i.e., his reserve price.[23]

---

[22] AGCOM (2019).

[23] In almost all markets, it is impossible to have such an outcome, as firms do not usually have such detailed information on their users and, therefore, charge an average price to all or implement some imperfect form of discrimination by quantities (second degree) or by users' groups (so that, whoever is willing to pay a higher price get a consumer surplus). In addition, where differentiated prices (e.g., low and high) and some competition exist, who buys at a low price could have an incentive to *arbitrage*, i.e., to resell the product to some consumers at a high price minus a tiny discount, subtracting consumers with a high reserve price. In foreseeing the arbitrage, the company would finally stop price discriminating. Instead, in the digital markets, 'almost perfect' price discrimination appears to be possible.

The business goal of the digital platforms is exactly that of mining private information and proposing, to each user, different offers based on what the platform algorithm calculates, at that precise moment, to be users' reserve price. In this way a platform could capture (almost) all consumers' surplus, and, at the same time, achieve the same aggregated allocative efficiency that a competitive market would reach, by selling a product or a service to all consumers having a willingness to pay equal or higher than the marginal cost of production.

As for economic theory, this outcome would produce an efficient allocation of resources, merely involving a redistributive effect, i.e., a transfer of economic resources from users to platforms. However, if one would weigh consumers' utility more than platforms' profits, then this outcome would not be neutral or anyway not completely socially desirable. This could be particularly true for policy makers, especially if they compare the redistributive impact on national consumers against the impact that platforms' profits have on national economy (e.g., investments, labour market, taxes). Nevertheless, within this simplified balancing assessment, it can't be disregarded that the counterfactual scenario (without platforms) is one where the enormous additional number of transactions allowed by platforms would not take place. Of course, as usual, some kind of redistributive policy intervention, "portioning the pie" in a different manner, could be desirable, yet being very careful of not (enormously) shrinking the overall size of that pie.

Moreover, as mentioned before, data and algorithms not only allow platforms to implement 'efficient' price discrimination but also to exponentially (a) improve their productive efficiency (minimising users' transaction and search costs/time) and (b) enhance the personalised quality of the service and product offered. In other words, users give to digital platforms data providing information on preferences on products, services, friends, news, political ideas, and visions of the world and platforms efficiently select and propose to them products, services, friends, news, political ideas, or vision of the world that (a) match their preferences and (b) save their search time (that is a scarce resource). At any moment, the supply aims to be the most efficient and most suitable response to users' demand.[24]

---

[24] Marciano et al. (2020).

Therefore, algorithmic price discrimination based on Big data is at the base of a double paradox: on one side, consumers satisfaction (in terms of preferences matching and better allocation of time) comes along with a reduction of consumer surplus; on the other side, an efficient allocation of resources, like in perfectly competitive market, comes along with the consumer being screened from competition, as the consumer's choice is increasingly restricted in a market segment, even though tailored on him, yet excluding all competitors.

As for the latter, the competitive problem is that price discrimination in a specific market is allowed by the extraction of informational rent appropriated exclusively by a single digital platform, which place consumers in a customised "information aftermarket".[25] In a sense, when a consumer choose a digital platform he also choose a *gatekeeper* that re-direct him towards an information aftermarket where the consumer is induced to exercise its freedom of choice within the limits and constraints decided by the gatekeeper itself, which pre-selects tailored offers based on information those platforms' algorithms can extrapolate from consumer's own data.

Moreover, users' data, and thus the algorithmic efficiency, comes also from users' time spent and activity done on a platform. In economic terms, along with Williamsonian approach, this could be considered a 'specific investments' made by users to increase efficiency of the service provided for free by the platforms. In this context, and considering the extremely incomplete contract between the user and the platform, notwithstanding the non-monetary transaction, platforms can lock-in users, by progressively asking for more and more data (in scale and scope) or additional 'consents' necessary to envelop them. Thus, the larger is the set of data released by users to the platforms, the higher is the users' exit cost from the platform (which appropriates a quasi-rent). Users do not seem able (or willing) to anticipate this kind of hold-up behavior, as this implicit exchange between data release and service access dissimulates the data transaction, the specific investment and the consequent (opportunity) costs for consumers to switch platforms.

---

[25] In economic theory, an *aftermarket* is a secondary market where consumers make their choices after having purchased a primary product or service, with an *ex-post* freedom of choice that is constrained by previous choices in the primary market (typical examples are complementary products and services, like maintenance, or consumable goods related to durable ones, like printer ink cartridge). See Hovenkamp (1994).

So, consumers get "locked-in" in a information aftermarket, where their freedom of choice and competition is limited within a single platform, which however tends to increasingly expand the scope of services offered. Indeed, one of the main things that the algorithms learn from our profiled data is indeed our predisposition to compare results on other platforms. So, price discrimination, capture of consumer's surplus and informational lock-in also depend on how 'lazy' consumers are.[26]

Indeed, the exit option from the gatekeeper will become less and less likely to happen, and not only because of the high opportunity costs generated by network externalities, but because consumers are less and less willing to compare other platforms' performance (multihoming) as "his" gatekeeper knows exactly his preferences and save him a lot of time. So, despite the possibility of multihoming, consumers allocate their time and attention relying on the platform that 'knows them better', from which they become progressively less and less willing to switch. Moreover, network externalities further magnify users' exit costs, at least as long as coordination costs (to switch towards an alternative platform) are higher than the expected benefits.

As a consequence, consumers continue to choose freely but within preselected tailored offers in restricted segments of the market, excluding competitors. It is true that these offers might be the 'most efficient and suitable choice' for the consumer, yet with an increasing complexity and customisation, the degree of comparability also get increasingly difficult. Hence, from this picture some economists foresee the 'end of markets' and competition dynamics, replaced by clusters (e.g., search engine, social networks, operating systems, app stores marketplaces) in which gatekeepers, powered by consumers' informational capture, are able to steer consumers' choice and exclude competition.[27]

So, is this 'end of the market' not so different to a classical monopolisation? And therefore, is data an 'essential asset' empowering platforms and allowing dominance or monopolistic power on the market? That's not completely the case.

First, in most cases platforms are not monopolies, as there are always at least few fringe competitors in the market. Second, all Big Techs can be considered to also be part of an oligopoly, competing in corner

---

[26] Patterson (2017).

[27] Odlyzko (2016).

markets that have not yet tipped over.[28] Moreover, there are certainly doubts about the possibility to consider data as a non-duplicable key asset, necessary to access the markets, as occurs for fixed telecommunication infrastructures and the other network industries, i.e., a proper essential facility or essential input.[29]

The reason for which big data are different from essential facilities has very much to do with the distinction of different kind of market failures. Indeed, as we have seen, the 'end of market' is a world of intense market power with limited or nil competition but also a place where companies have perfect market information and use it to decide what are products and services susceptible to be bought by each consumer in each moment at a certain price. This does not happen in a classical monopoly context, where a monopolist is more than dominant, hegemonic, but still doesn't own and control in an exclusive way the whole market informative resources and dynamics.

5.3   COMPETITION FOR (BEING) THE MARKET AND DATA PROPERTY RIGHTS

The ideal–typical market, depicted as a place for free exchange in the history of economic thought, effectively allows all market players—companies, consumers, workers—to be better off, should no restrictions on trading take place (*laissez faire, laissez passer*).

To explain why this happens, Adam Smith elaborated the renowned metaphor of the "invisible hand"—an ideal hand steering people and moving things, goods and resources, so that at the end of all exchanges and transactions each one is satisfied, because self-interested actions have produced an (unintended) social desirable outcome.[30] Adam Smith's invisible hand was widely recognised as an early informal description of the fact that free market dynamics, in a perfectly competitive context,

---

[28] Petit (2020).

[29] Many supporters of the Scumpeterian vision of digital markets are of the opinion that Big Data should not be considered an insurmountable barrier to market entry. There would exist, according to this theory, a threshold beyond which data has a decreasing return to scale and scope, getting finally to a situation in which collecting further data give a nil marginal advantage. This situation of course would give much less relevance to the quantity of data—and platform scale and scope—as an entry barrier.

[30] Smith (1776).

lead to an efficient allocation of resources[31] and to a maximisation of the net social benefit.

Another eminent economist, Léon Walras, explained how the invisible hand produces this efficient and socially desirable outcome. Walras replaced the metaphor of the invisible hand with that of an ideal "auctioneer", who receives all private offers on the selling and buying prices which appear on the market and then set the equilibrium prices for the efficient exchanges.[32]

Finally, Friedrich von Hayek specified that both metaphors, the invisible hand as well as the auctioneer ones, actually describe the capacity of market competition to reveal, with no costs, information otherwise (uselessly) lost.[33] Searching for the best prices to buy or the buyers willing to pay a higher price are costly activities, as they require time, moving about, advertising investments, market surveys, and so on. As a matter of fact, in the neoclassic vision of the market, the competitive mechanism (i.e., decentralised competition between companies and free choice of consumers) works better than all the possible alternatives as it collects and reveals all the dispersed information, reducing to zero transaction and searching costs and time. Once the information is revealed, it becomes a public good, because the exchanges and equilibrium prices are observable for all (information is both non-excludable and non-rivalrous[34]) and are

---

[31] According to welfare economics standard results, a general economic equilibrium in a competitive market—where consumers and businesses maximise their utility functions— produces an allocation of resources for which it is impossible to increase the welfare of one individual without diminishing the welfare of another individual (Pareto efficiency—Allocative efficiency). Market failures are those situations whereby this welfare economics result does not hold, i.e., situations of market power, externalities, public good, asymmetric information and market incompleteness.

[32] Walras (1900) and Walras (1954).

[33] Von Hayek (1978).

[34] Information is a public good in that: (a) its consumption (or access to) by a subject does not mean that another subject cannot use it at the same time (non-rivalry consumption); (b) once produced, it is difficult to stop other subjects who haven't paid from using it (non-excludability consumption). In theory, the information can be consumed infinitely and by a multitude of subjects, and the ability to exclude third-party access depends on many factors. For example, the introduction of copyright confers a temporary full property rule, on the author for a certain number of years before becoming a public good. In these cases, the economic ratio lies in remunerating the creativity of the intellectual work. However, according to many scholars, there is nothing creative in the data of our digital footprint and, therefore, it belongs to the public domain, which we can all access due to

used by each player to take productive and commercial decision aimed to increase its utility/profits, producing in this way an increase in the overall allocative efficiency.

Here we come to the point: Smith's, Walras' and Von Hayek's ideas seem to come about, all together, in digital markets, where transaction and information search costs are close to zero and information is almost perfect.[35] However, this information in digital markets is absolutely not observable for all. Platforms do not reveal information to the different sides of the markets but internalise it and transform it into an exclusive informational rent. In this way, digital platforms do not only try to expand their power in the market but attempt to become, themselves, the market, with its power to collect all disperse private information, yet retaining all the information.

This is indeed a market failure, which is however inherently different from market power. The latter, instead, may be not an actual market failure for digital platform, because of their ability to perfectly discriminate, and therefore producing an efficient allocation of resources, avoiding a deadweight loss (yet, according to many, unfair because of appropriation of all consumer surplus). On the contrary, internalisation of market information goes to the core of competitive market functioning, and deeply alters it. In this sense, digital platforms' power and prominence is not the result of replicable Schumpeterian dynamics that have risen in free competitive markets, but a much more permanent power (absent public intervention) where platforms works as the new institution, replacing the market (and somehow also regulators).[36] That's why, generally speaking, it is more accurate to talk about Big Techs' economic power rather than market power.

So, from the Schumpeterian concept of 'creative destruction', that is the substitutability and cyclical substitution of leading companies 'in' the

the simple fact that this data has been revealed. However, this thesis, supported by, among others, Néstor Duch-Brown, Bertin Martens and Frank Mueller-Langer (2017), clashes with the fact that this public data is not always released in a public environment and, once released, becomes in an exclusive use, through a proxy consent, which is acquired solely for the purpose of advertising profiling.

[35] See Posner and Weyl (2018).

[36] As already seen, the joint use of more the one online platform by users (multihoming) could in part, and under certain conditions, mitigate this situation. However, as the European Commission revealed in the Google Search case, the level of multihoming still does not appear to have reached a point of counteracting the big tech market power.

market, digital platforms go toward the substitutability and substitution of a leading company 'with' the market. Indeed becoming "the market" is a very effective way not to be substituted in the market and break the Schumpeterian cycle. In other words, there is not a competition in the market, and not only a competition for the market, yet a competition for being the market.[37] This locution highlights both the tendency of competition to result in a monopoly-like market structure,[38] and the fact that this (institutional) structure is de facto privatised, and hierarchically centralised, i.e., the platform. In this context, competition law intervention may not be effective in re-establishing competitive dynamics, and, for the very same reason, a big data owner is different from an essential facility owner.

At the same time, a public good (information) *de facto* becomes privately owned and is exploited only by the platform which has, for various purposes, the users' privacy consent for the exclusive use of the data. In this context, also privacy and data protection rules may not be effective, and may even have a secondary unintended effect, working as a monopoly (legal) guarantee upon the economic use of the data. Indeed, data protection does not eliminate, as some mistakenly believe, data economic exploitation by platforms, but only ends up removing data, as an economic good, from the market. In short, this could thus create a conflict between (a) safeguarding privacy by consents and exclusive data use, and (b) the existence of the economic value extracted by third parties in an exclusive way, which is detrimental for competition in the digital ecosystem.

In the next section, the policy debate about the establishment of an ex-ante pro-competitive regulatory framework is outlined. Nevertheless, a (complementary) solution based on decentralised market forces disciplining platforms seems to be possible and desirable. As often happens, that is based on consumers empowerment, in this case, by better defining property rights of each user on its own data. This could enable market forces to address the core neglected market failures previously described, i.e., private market information and the implicit transaction between data and free services.

---

[37] Marciano et al. (2020).

[38] Consistently with the traditional meaning of competition for the market, which refers to definition of new dominant standards or business models tending to a monopoly market structure. Geroski (2003).

To explain this, we must refer to another economist, Ronald Coase, who explained that when markets à la Hayek don't work because there are high transactions costs for setting prices, firms would tend to internalise those transactions and relationships.[39] In this sense, firms and their hierarchical centralised relationships are remedies to a market failure. Also two-sided digital platforms are mechanisms to remedy a market failure by addressing (i.e., internalising) those externalities and high transaction costs necessary to (efficiently) match and connect different groups of market players.

In this framework, large digital platforms however aim to centralise and internalise also the transaction between data and (free) services that takes place on the user side of the platforms, by making it organic to its overall relationships with users and thus making it implicit. This implicit exchange happens within a contractual framework, inherently incomplete, where platforms have much stronger bargaining and renegotiation powers. Therefore, the relationship between users, or data providers/subjects, and platforms is very similar to a centralised organic relationship within a firm.

For platforms, besides expanding their user bases by adopting zero-price strategies, the main rationale for implicit data exchange is to dissimulate: that's a method (a) not to reveal information about data as an economic good (i.e., price, willingness to pay, quantity) and (b) not to emphasise the very existence of a data market. Data, as an economic good, has a demand and a supply and produces value. The fact that supply and demand has been internalised within a vertically integrated organisational structure (and data asset are held exclusively by those who have received the consent) does not mean at all that there is not a (potential) market for that input.

As a matter of fact, in the digital world it would be very much possible to set data prices with very low transaction costs, via algorithmic consumer empowerment.[40] Therefore, it is not necessary to internalise those transaction in an organic relationship, on the contrary, a centralisation/internalisation creates here additional transaction costs. This is exactly as inefficient as a vertical integration in a situation where market and decentralised interactions could be efficiently used. Obviously, on

---

[39] Coase (1937).

[40] That's exactly the job carried out by some software and apps.

the company side, if there are quasi-monopolistic rents, renouncing to a centralised relationship leads to an opportunity cost in terms of rent dissipation, and maybe in terms of productive efficiency. However, social welfare would turn out to be enhanced.

A transparent and well-functioning data market would be therefore the most effective solution. Nevertheless, creating a data market is quite problematic, since data, as an economic good, is pervasively ambiguous as its property rights, in current legal systems, are inherently incomplete.[41] Having a property right means that the owner has entitlements that can be the object of specific economic transactions. Indeed, innovation has always produced tension within existing property rights, modifying them, and generating incompleteness insofar it become unclear what entitlements are included.

According to another lesson of Ronald Coase, condition to have a well-functioning market is that goods must have well-defined property rights, which can then be exchanged on the market and the market will then be able to resolve conflicts between different parties as they arise (externalities).[42] If, instead, the cost of using markets as institutions is too high, it could be more efficient to resolve any possible problems through private coordination (a firm) or public regulation of private rights.

The exchange of data, beyond a clear definition of property rights, technically creates a situation of market failure—that is, the inability of the market to autonomously generate an optimal level of production and its efficient allocation. Moreover, within this implicit exchange process, a further paradox emerges: an entitlement to certain uses of information originates and is recognised only after the transaction, but only for those who receive it, i.e., platforms, which exclusively use it, extract and appropriate an economic value from it. Whereas before the transaction personal data is not endowed by any property right to the person who generated that information.

As a matter of facts, according to the traditional legal interpretation of personal data, which has been carried over from the pre-digital world, data rights are not property rights, since they are inalienable, as a non-negotiable essential part of our being. We can delegate its management for a specific use, but only for certain purposes and in a way to limit

---

[41] Demsetz (1967, 1998) and Nicita et al. (2007).

[42] Coase (1960)

treatments and discolsures. This explains the origin of digital privacy protection as a guarantee of the inalienability and non-negotiability of personal data.

In the digital era, however, this interpretation of personal data (unfortunately) appears to be illusory. In practice, despite data protection, the public good nature of information makes it increasingly more difficult to exclude e-commerce platforms, cloud computing operators, social networks, search engines and so on, from gathering and using citizen-users digital data. This is even more true, when data are collected outside any contractual relationship, as in the IoT.[43] Then the use of data by those who receive it, as we have seen, is an input to carry out an economic transaction in another sphere, for example, offering profiled advertising space to advertisers. Therefore, the valorisation of the data is a by-product of the service offered to the user.

So, a radical yet non-intrusive way to solve the problem would be to define (complete) property rights (power of control) over the data, or better over some uses of the data itself instead of the (old) principle of data consent that remains non-negotiable. Some uses could thus remain in the personal domain, as non-disposable (e.g., transferring a person's name), others could belong to the public domain (aggregated data for traffic, environmental protection, health policies and so on), whereas some others could be subject to explicit market transactions and bargaining. In the last case, relevant property rights or entitlements would be established for some data uses, so that an explicit and transparent market transaction could take place. These would not lose their 'personal-right' nature, as the original owner of that data would be the person who has generated it and who would, therefore, maintain its full (residual right of) control. Nevertheless, under an economic perspective, would be treated as a right of publicity:[44] for example as a personal image and its right of economic exploitation.[45]

---

[43] There are numerous examples of data and image mining that occur outside a contractual and consent relationship, with the data originators being fully unaware of it.

[44] The right of publicity gives people the right to control the use of their names and likenesses for commercial purposes. Dogan and Lemley (2005) and Grady (1994).

[45] A similar outcome is achievable by applying IP law to personal data, see Trakman et al. (2019).

Well-defined data property rights, on the one hand, would avoid the *de facto* appropriation and exploitation of the data arising only when falling into the hands of those who have received the consent to use it, returning it back, instead, to the user, the data subjects to whom data refers. On the other hand, it would also resolve the potential conflict between privacy protection and safeguarding competition, leaving to the data owner the formal and substantive choice to arrange the use of their data, for example, by granting it to third parties for a limited period. The right of data portability (Sect. 4.4) already somehow responds to this logic.

Finally, well-defined data property rights would make a digital data transaction and bargaining explicit, as building-blocks of an actual transparent data market, which could finally emerge. This simple outcome would be an incredible overall improvement for the development of effective public policies and regulatory remedies, so enabled to address core market failures.

REFERENCES

AGCOM. (2019). *Report on online platforms*.

Baker, J. (2019). *The antitrust paradigm*. Harvard University Press.

Bork, R. H. (1978). *The antitrust paradox: A policy at war with itself*. Basic Books.

Coase, R. (1960). The problem of social cost. *Journal of Law and Economics, 3,* 1–44.

Coase, R. (1937). The nature of the firm. *Economica, 4*(16), 386–405.

Crémer, J., De Montjoye, Y.-A., & Schweitzer, H. (2019). *Competition policy for the digital era*. A Report for the European Commission.

Cunningham, C., Ederer, F., & Ma, S. (2021). Killer acquisitions. *Journal of Political Economy, 129*(3), 649–702.

Demsetz, H. (1967). Toward a theory of property rights. *American Economic Review, 57*(2), 347–359.

Demsetz, H. (1998). Property rights. In *The new Palgrave dictionary of economics and the law* (pp. 144–155). Palgrave Macmillan.

Dogan, S. L., & Lemley, M. A. (2005). What the right of publicity can learn from trademark law. *Stanford Law Review, 58,* 1161–1220.

Duch-Brown, N., Martens, B., & Mueller-Lange F. (2017). The economics of ownership, access and trade in digital data. *JRC Digital Economy Working Paper. 2017–01.*

Eisenmann, T. (2006). *Winner-take-all in networked markets* (Background Note). Harvard Business School.

Eisenmann, T., Parker, G., & Van Alstyne, M. (2011). Platform envelopment. *Strategic Management Journal, 32*(12), 1270–1285.

Evans, D., & Schmalensee, R. (2016). *Matchmakers: The new economics of multisided*. Harvard Business Review Press

Furman, J., Coyle, D., Fletcher, A., Marsden, P., & D. McAuley (2019). *Unlocking digital competition*. British Digital Competition Expert Panel.

Gautier, A., & Lamesch, J. (2020). *Mergers in the digital economy* (CESifo Working Paper No. 8056). Available at SSRN: https://ssrn.com/abstract= 3529012

Geroski, P. (2003). Competition in markets and competition for markets. *Journal of Industry, Competition and Trade, 3*, 151–166.

Grady, M. (1994). A positive economic theory of the right of publicity. *UCLA Entertainment Law Review, 1*, 97.

Hovenkamp, H. (1994). *Federal antitrust policy: The law of competition and its practice*. West Group Ed.

Hovenkamp, H. (2021). Antitrust and platform monopoly. *Yale Law Journal, 130*, 8.

Khan, L. (2016). Amazon's antitrust paradox. *Yale Law Journal, 126*.

Khan, L. (2018). The ideological roots of America's market power problem. *Yale Law Journal Forum, 127*, 960.

Latham O., Tecu I., & Bagaria N. (2020, May). *Beyond killer acquisitions: Are there more common potential competition issues in tech deals and how can these be assessed?* Competition Policy International, Antitrust Chronicle.

Marciano, A., Nicita, A., & Ramello, G. B. (2020). Big data and big techs: Understanding the value of information in platform capitalism. *European Journal of Law and Economics, 50*, 345–358.

Motta, M., & Peitz, M. (2021). Big tech mergers. *Information Economics and Policy, 54*.

Nicita, A., Rossi M. A., Rizzolli, M. (2007). *Towards a theory of incomplete property rights*. American Law & Economics Association Annual Meetings, n. 42.

Odlyzko, A. M. (2016). The growth rate and nature of Internet traffic. *Transactions on Internet Research*. Special issue on New Developments on the Web, *12*(1), 39–42.

OECD. (2020). *Start-ups, killer acquisitions and merger control* (Background Note). DAF/COMP(2020).

Patterson, M. (2017). *Antitrust law in the new economy: Google, Yelp. LIBOR, and the control of information*. Harvard University Press.

Petit, N. (2020). *Big tech and the digital economy: The moligopoly scenario*. Oxford University Press.

Posner, E. A., & Weyl, G. (2018) *Radical markets: Uprooting capitalism and democracy for a just society.* Princeton University Press.

Posner, R. (2001) *Antitrust law.* University of Chicago Press.

Prat, A., & Valletti, Attention Oligopoly (May 25, 2021). *American Economic Journal: Microeconomics,* Forthcoming, Available at SSRN: https://ssrn.com/abstract=3197930.

Schumpeter, J. A. (1934). *The theory of economic development.* Cambridge University Press.

Shy, O. (2001). *The economics of network industries.* Cambridge University Press.

Smith, A. (1776). *An inquiry into the nature and causes of the wealth of nations* (Book IV, Chapter 8, 49). Methuen & Co.

Tirole, J. (2020). *Competition and the industrial challenge for the digital age.* Available at: https://www.tse-fr.eu/sites/default/files/TSE/documents/doc/by/tirole/competition_and_the_industrial_challenge_april_3_2020.pdf

Trakman, L., Walters, R., & Zeller, B. (2019). Is privacy and personal data set to become the new intellectual property? *IIC, 50,* 937–970.

Von Hayek, F. (1978). Competition as a discovery procedure. In F. A. von Hayek (Ed.), *New studies in philosophy, politics, economics and the history of ideas* (pp. 179–190). Chicago University Press.

Walras, L. (1900). *Éléments d'économie politique pure.* Routledge.

Walras, L. (1954). *Elements of pure economics* (translation of the fifth edition by W Jaffé).

Wu, T. (2018). *The curse of bigness: Antitrust in the new gilded age.* Columbia Global Reports.

CHAPTER 6

Regulating Big Techs and Their Economic Power

Abstract Competition law enforcement has taken the lead on public intervention in digital markets, mainly due to its enforcement flexibility and ability to adapt to new market circumstances. Nevertheless, it has been perceived by many to be too slow and not completely effective. Based on these arguments, there has been a world-wide intense public policy debate on how to tackle the overall competitive and consumer issues in digital platform economy, and what could be the most effective policy for data economy. As a result, the EU Commission has proposed a few crucial policy actions, such as the Data Governance Act (DGA), the Data Act, the Digital Services Act (DSA) and the Digital Markets Act (DMA). The latter is based on a 'codification' of competition case-law in order to improve enforceability by implementing ex-ante regulation, which however may not adequately consider the heterogeneity of the Core Platform Services and the different 'gatekeeper' platforms' business models. Nevertheless, the DMA tackles some of the main concerns within digital markets, particularly about the use and access of data. Indeed, rules about data portability, interoperability and empowerment of end-users (also via data intermediaries) could address the main digital market failures, and progressively enable a *ne[x]t neutrality* future-proof approach for the entire digital ecosystem.

© The Author(s), under exclusive license to Springer Nature Switzerland AG 2022
A. Manganelli and A. Nicita, *Regulating Digital Markets*,
Palgrave Studies in Institutions, Economics and Law,
https://doi.org/10.1007/978-3-030-89388-0_6

Keywords Big Techs' power · Competition Law · Regulation · EU digital and data Policies · Digital Markets Act

6.1   COMPETITION LAW OR REGULATION? WHAT KIND OF COMPLEMENTARITY AND SELECTIVE INTERVENTION?

Big Techs' exploitation of data (as outlined in Sects. 5.2 and 5.3) is based on three main features:

a. transactions are based on implicit exchange of data for cheap or free services in a multi-sided market context;
b. these transactions have a material impact on consumers' transaction and search costs, which allow to reach cost-efficient outcomes;
c. dispersed and decentralised information, 'revealed' in online market transactions, ceases to be a public good, i.e., perfectly observable by everyone, as it is (de facto) internalised and exploited by (vertically and horizontally) integrated large platforms in order to become "the market".

Getting closer to quasi-monopolistic markets, i.e., having all possible subscribers, and embracing more and more markets, the larger platforms get larger and larger sets of customers data, thus getting the ability to identify preferences and willingness to pay of each customer and thus perfectly discriminate price, quality, and supply. This circle of efficiency, and consequent increase in scale, affects users' incentives to "trade" more and more data in the implicit exchange with services and to remain inert as consumers, locked-in an "information digital aftermarket".

Whether competitors can break such a "loop" is a complex issue and depends on whether innovation can overcome a data disadvantage and what type of innovation can do it.

In order to individuate and assess digital platform economic power, certain conditions must be evaluated[1]:

a. the nature and other characteristics of the data collected;

---

[1] Stucke and Grunes (2016).

b. the efficiency of the algorithms (which, in turn, depend on the characteristics of the data);
c. the network economies (that increase the cost-opportunity of leaving the platform for users, where it would be difficult to find the same advantages in another platform);
d. the economies of scale (allowing the platform to reduce participation costs thanks to its size);
e. the economies of scope (allowing the platform to reduce costs on supply linked to services);
f. the existing coordination costs that the users should bear when abandoning the current platform and migrating to a competitor, to maintain the same network impact;
g. the lack of interoperability (that increases the platform loyalty and limits competitive or complementary service companies from entering the market);
h. the lack of data transferability (that increases both the user exit cost from the platform and the entry cost of a new operator).

All these aspects must be weighed and combined in order to understand whether a platform is 'dominant' in a market context. Big data driven platforms are often described as dominant because of their importance and their global dimension, and their economies of scale regarding supply and demand. However, it remains quite difficult to identify which are the targeted relevant markets, given the nature of the intermediaries among more markets and more sides.

As a matter of facts, as a prerequisite for the identification of market power and then dominance, the regulator must define a 'relevant market'.

A relevant market is defined according to both product and geographic factors. A relevant product market comprises all those products and/or services which are regarded as interchangeable or substitutable by consumers by reason of the products' characteristics, their prices and their intended use; whereas a relevant geographic market comprises the area in which the firms concerned are involved in the supply of products or services and in which the conditions of competition are sufficiently homogeneous.

One of the main theoretical points in the economics of the digital ecosystem is about redefining the notion of relevant market and, more generally, how the competitive dynamics evolve. Indeed, competition is constantly reshaped by innovative processes and appears to become, from the geographical point of view, increasingly global and, from the product point of view, increasingly cross-market and conglomerate (touching upon further dimensions other than the typical horizontal and vertical ones we usually use to describe competitive and organisational phenomena).[2]

The main dilemma here is based on the fact that, usually, antitrust authorities and regulators must assess market dynamics quickly, before any concrete effect is observable into the market. Which brings them to choose between increasing the risk of false positives (i.e., intervening now on market power positions that will turn out to be unharmful for the market, thus hurting innovation) and the risk of false negatives (i.e., not intervening on market power situation which will escalate and will be difficult to be contended by new entrants)—not being able to know *ex-ante* which of these risks is greater and has a greater probability of occurring.

In these circumstances and uncertainty, competition law enforcement usually has the first moves, due to its higher flexibility and possibility to quickly adapt to marginal evolution of the market. Nevertheless, when radical and disruptive transformation are involved, a new ad-hoc regulatory framework may be the best policy. Here is where the dilemma come out again, and under an institutional perspective has taken the form of the policy debate about the relationship between competition law enforcement and regulation, and what is the best suited policy tool for addressing the competitive problems and market failures of the large global digital platforms.

Moreover, considering the existing antitrust and regulatory approaches, an additional crucial policy dilemma is whether it is necessary to rethink the typical antitrust and regulation tools so as to adapt them to the digital ecosystem challenges, or policy makers and regulators can still rely on "traditional" tools and mechanisms.

As a general consideration, if the digital ecosystem is still exposed to potential competition (or forthcoming competition), exactly as it happened for *Netscape* and *Microsoft*, then a *soft regulation* approach, along with competition law enforcement and deterrence, perhaps rethinking and progressively adjusting some of its typical intervention tools and principles, would probably be the optimal policy choice. On the contrary, if the monopolistic power is consolidated and institutionalised,

---

[2] Bourreau and de Streel (2019).

as envisioned in the previous section, an ad-hoc regulatory framework seems to be necessary to tackle those specific market failures involved, while stand-alone antitrust intervention, at least in its traditional form,[3] would not be able to overcome the competitive problems.

For a few years, there has been a deep debate in Europe, and worldwide, in order to answer those questions, and specifically if and how to develop some legislative reforms in order to approach and tackle online platforms and big tech market, bargaining and economic power (Box 6.1). At the end, it emerged a large consensus that existing competition law is able to tackle only a small part of the antitrust issues concerning large digital platforms, and there are conflicting opinions about its effectiveness. First, the EC looked at a substantial reform of competition law, in order to overcome its (perceived) substantial and procedural pitfalls when applied to large digital platforms (e.g., the market definition, the identification of a clear theory of harm, standard of proof, timing, merger control's thresholds, etc.). Eventually, as described in the next Sect. 6.3, the EC has proposed an ex-ante regulatory regime, in which it extends the scope and concepts of the P2B regulation (Sect. 4.3) in order to ensure that digital markets where gatekeepers operate, are fair and contestable throughout the whole EU.

Box 6.1 Public Reports on Digital Strategies

In order to provide policy makers with new useful guidance about public policy in digital markets, a number task forces around the world were established in recent years, among those: the EU Commission experts' panel,[4] the German ad-hoc Commission 'Competition Law 4.0',[5] the British Digital Competition Experts Panel (Furman Report),[6] the Stigler Committee for the Study of

---

[3] As many scholars claim, the typical tools of antitrust and regulation need to be adapted to meet the challenges of the digital ecosystem, for example Tirole (2020) and Colangelo (2020).

[4] Crémer et al. (2019).

[5] Schallbruch et al. (2019).

[6] Furman et al. (2019).

Digital Platforms (University of Chicago)[7] and the joint report delivered by the Italian Authorities for Antitrust (AGCM), Electronic Communications & Media (AGCOM) and Data protection (GPDP).[8] Moreover, other interesting documents were delivered by the UK Competition and Markets Authority (CMA)[9] and the Australian Competition and Consumer Commission (ACCC) in the realm of their 'markets regime' powers.[10] In their very essence, all these reports deal with four main issues: (a) the need to update the competition law enforcement toolbox, (b) ex-ante regulation tailored on platform-based largest companies, (c) new regulatory strategies fostering data sharing and interoperability, and (d) some implications on the public bodies' institutional design.

As for competition law enforcement, several proposals emerged. According to the EU Commission report, less emphasis should be put on the market definition, whereas more importance should be attributed to the theories of harm and identification of anti-competitive strategies. The interdependence of the markets becomes a crucial part, and the zero-price side of a platform can be part of a market insofar there is some forms of exchange.[11] Another crucial flaw of competition policy is under-enforcement, which is a particular concern in the digital era, as the harm will presumably be longer term than in traditional markets because of the enduring market power. Therefore, even if the consumer harm cannot be precisely measured, any conduct excluding competitors or tending to restrict competition by dominant platforms should be forbidden in the absence of clearly documented consumer welfare gains. Thus, the European report calls for a modification of the burden of proof in order to shift on the defendant to show pro-competitiveness of the conduct at issue by complying with the standard of proof.

[7] Stigler Committee for the Study of Digital Platforms (2019).

[8] AGCM et al. (2019).

[9] CMA (2019).

[10] ACCC (2019).

[11] pp. 44–55.

For its part, the German Commission emphasises the need to update the Commission Notice on the definition of the relevant market, in relation to the relevance of multi-sidedness of digital platforms, lock-in effects, the limits of the SSNIP test in case of zero-price (side of) markets and the relevance of innovation spaces (rather than markets). Further, the German ad-hoc Commission calls for greater use of flexible, targeted remedies, with a particular focus on restorative remedies (e.g. the obligation of a dominant company to establish technical interoperability by disclosing interface information or to grant data access may be of particular importance in the digital economy—even in cases where the infringement of competition did not consist in an abusive refusal of interoperability or data access). According to the Stigler Committee's Study, it is time for antitrust law to recalibrate the balance it strikes between the risks of false positives and false negatives. Antitrust law might be revised to relax the proof requirements imposed upon antitrust plaintiffs in appropriate cases or to reverse burdens of proof, for example, by adopting rules that will presume anticompetitive harm on the basis of preliminary showings by antitrust plaintiffs or by ensuring that plaintiffs are not required to prove matters to which the defendants have greater knowledge and better access to relevant information.

As for ex ante regulation of platforms, emphasis is placed on new specific rules of conduct. According to the EU Commission report, because of the rule-setting role of platforms, dominant platforms have a special responsibility to ensure that competition on their platforms is fair, unbiased, and pro-users. This responsibility is even more needed in the case of platforms that play a dual role, i.e., at the same operate marketplaces and sell their own products and/or services on these marketplaces. Remarkably, intermediation power—and hence regulatory power—can exist even where the market share is significantly below 40%.[12] On this point, the German ad-hoc Commission focuses mainly on preserving the contestability of

---

[12] See Schweitzeret et al. (2018): a lowering of the intervention threshold for controlling abuse is recommended for specific groups of cases. In markets which tend to "tip", unilateral conduct that could promote the tipping of the market should be prohibited even below the threshold for dominance. In addition, the "intermediation power" which

dominant digital platforms as well as on strengthening the position of consumers by protecting their ability to make meaningful choices and to determine how their data are processed and used. Therefore, it proposes the development of new rules of conduct for dominant digital platforms (with a certain level of revenues or a certain number of users) through an EU Platform Regulation that supplements competition law, complementing the P2B Regulation by exceeding its transparency obligations but limited to dominant players, and sets clear-cut prohibitions (rather than standards) for dominant online platforms, with a possibility for them to prove that an exception is justified. Notably, the British Digital Competition Experts put forward a new 'dominance' category: companies with strategic market status, meaning those firms in a position to exercise market power over a gateway or bottleneck in a digital market, where they control others' market access, i.e., with enduring market power over a strategic bottleneck market. According to the British report, pro-competition regulation of such players would sustain and promote effective competition in digital markets. To this aim, a digital markets unit (DMU) within the CMA should be entrusted with the task of imposing regulatory measures where a company holds a strategic market status. Accordingly, the CMA's market study interim report on Online Platforms and Digital Advertising proposed to develop a pro-competitive regulatory regime for online platforms funded by digital advertising. In the same vein, the joint report from the Italian Authorities outlines the need to reduce information asymmetries between digital corporations/platforms and their users. Such goal could be achieved also through antitrust law by considering factors other than price and quantity (such as quality, innovation, and fairness). On a similar note, the ACCC proposes to reform privacy law and consumer law, introducing specific prohibitions against unfair contract terms and certain unfair trading practices, in order to address the imbalance of bargaining power between digital platforms and consumers and

---

platforms may have as intermediaries under certain circumstances should be defined in the law as a separate third form of market power, in addition to the conventional categories of supply-side and demand-side power.

the ability of consumers to both be informed about their data and exercise control over it.

As for data sharing, all the proposals aim at facilitating interoperability and access for consumers and businesses through sector specific rules. In order to overcome particularly pronounced lock-in effects, the EU Commission experts' panel advocates an access regimes for data through sector-specific regulation (as in the context of the PSD2 Directive)—in particular where data access opens up secondary markets for complementary services. Similarly, the German ad-hoc Commission proposes the development of sector-specific rules on access to data and data portability obligation for dominant platforms: dominant online platforms that fall under the scope of the Platform Regulation should be required to enable for their users the portability of data in real time and to ensure interoperability with complementary services. In particular, for the German panel there is a case for imposing additional duties upon dominant platforms to grant partial protocol interoperability (the ability of two services or products to interconnect, technically, with one another) and data interoperability (a continuous, potentially real-time, access to personal or machine user data).

Under an institutional viewpoint, the British Digital Competition Expert Panel and the Stigler Committee argue that a Digital Authority could be a valuable complement to antitrust enforcement. This new entity should define digital platforms' codes of conduct, oversee personal data mobility and systems with open standards, thus creating "light touch" rules (behavioural nudges) that can lead consumers to make better choices and pursue data openness as a tool to increase competition. Conversely, the German report is "against the idea of establishing a public utilities-style regulation for the digital economy"; however, to promote a stronger cross-sectoral information collection, the German Panel is open to establish a Digital Markets Board within its General Secretariat as well as a Digital Markets Transformation Agency at the EU level, which should be entrusted with collection and processing of information about market developments and coordination of Member States' actions. On a different note, the Australian inquiry does not recommend the establishment of a new regulatory authority but to create a specialist digital platforms branch within the ACCC. Regardless of the institutional model adopted, the Italian joint report stresses the importance of a "permanent coordination" between all public bodies involved (i.e., AGCM, AGCOM and GPDP in Italy) because an effective policy for Big Data and digital economy should be grounded not only on law enforcement but also on coherent advocacy activities.

6.2   Shaping Europe's Digital Economy and Data Strategy

Following that extensive global debate described in the previous section, at the end of 2020 the EU Commission started better defining its overall digital and data strategy. In the Communication "Shaping Europe's digital future" the EC lays out the main pillars of next five-year policy strategy.[13] In 2021, the EU Commission, with the Communication "Digital compass 2030" extended its sight to the next decade, presenting visions, targets, and setting out those paths to be followed towards digital transformation of Europe by 2030.[14]

The latter Communication aims to set out the EU way for digital transformation around four cardinal points: (a) Deployment of secure and high-performing digital infrastructures; (b) Digital transformation of businesses; (c) Development of digital skills and literacy; and (d) Digitalisation of core public services (e-government, e-health). The digital compass is thus focused on the EU Digital citizenship, concerning digital rights and principles to be applied in the digital market society.

The 2020 Communication specifically deals also with platforms competition and regulation. The key points are:

a. citizens empowerment through facilitated forms of data control and data sharing within the Internal Market.[15] Therefore, all firms

[13] European   Commission (2020a).

[14] European   Commission (2021)

[15] European   Commission (2020a).

(whether public or private, big or small, start-up or giant) should be able to access data on a level playing field,[16] by setting consistent rules for companies and "stronger mechanisms for proactive information-sharing".[17] In the same vein, the EU intends to pursue an "EU governments interoperability strategy" to ensure coordination and common standards for secure and borderless public sector data flows and services. By so doing, the EC aims to build a "European data space" where the value created by data-enabled services and products is shared back with consumers and society. Finally, the EC wants to enable consumers with a universally accepted public electronic identity (eID) allowing them to have access to their data and securely use the products and services they want without having to use unrelated platforms to do so and unnecessarily sharing personal data with them.[18]

b. As for Big Tech, the EU acknowledges that some platform-based companies managed to acquire significant scale, enabling them to act "as private gatekeepers to markets, customers and information".[19] Therefore, it is fundamental that platforms' economic power is not harmful for fairness and openness of European markets. It is key that competition law remains up to the task of dealing with the challenges of digital markets. Moreover, the EC recognised that competition policy alone cannot address all the systemic problems that may arise in the platform economy. So, there is the need of an effective ex-ante regulatory framework, where all kinds of rules (tax, consumer protection, etc.) applicable to digital services across the EU are strengthened and modernised, clarifying the roles and responsibilities of online platforms.[20]

As for (b), in order to create a protected digital ecosystem for users of digital services and to establish a level playing field to foster innovation,

---

[16] European Commission (2020a): "a level playing field for businesses, big and small, is more important than ever. This suggests that rules applying offline – from competition and single market rules, consumer protection, to intellectual property, taxation and workers' rights – should also apply online".

[17] European Commission (2020a).

[18] European Commission (2020a).

[19] European Commission (2020a).

[20] European Commission (2020a).

growth, and competitiveness, the EU Commission proposed two legislative initiatives to upgrade rules governing digital players in the EU, in order to complement competition law: the Digital Markets Act (DMA), and the Digital Services Act (DSA),which will be respectively described and analysed in Sect. 6.3 and Sect. 7.5 to create a safer digital space in which the fundamental rights of all users of digital services are protected.

As for the data strategy (a), the EU Commission issued an additional specific thematic Communication,[21] acknowledging that today "a small number of Big Tech firms hold a large part of the world's data".[22] This could reduce the incentives for data-driven businesses to surface, flourish, and innovate in the EU market. However, according to the EC, things are set to change as a large part of the data of the future will come from industrial and professional applications rather than data centres and centralised computing facilities managed by foreign Big Tech companies.[23] EC intends to design a policy strategy that avoids concentration effects, while preserving high privacy, security, safety, and ethical standards—thereby marking a clear difference from the Chinese model.

Indeed (a) and (b) are strictly interrelated policies. As highlighted in Sects. 5.2 and 5.3, gatekeeper's power is based onto strong market imbalances in relation to access to and use of data. As underlined, big online platforms are able to gather and harness large amounts of data thereby drawing insights and competitive advantages over SMEs. In turn, platform providers are leveraging their gatekeeper role to entrench and extend their market power. As a consequence, they are getting always more difficult to contest by potential competitors.[24]

An open and dynamic European Data Space is going to be at the centre of the EU data strategy for the next years. It would be characterised by smooth forms of data sharing among consumers and businesses, effective implementation of EU rules (in particular competition law, data protection law and consumer protection) and international data flows

---

[21] European Commission (2020b) Communication EU data strategy.

[22] European Commission (2020b).

[23] The EC points out that, by 2025, 20% of the processing and analysis of data will take place in data centres and centralised computing facilities, and 80% in smart connected objects, such as cars, home appliances or manufacturing robots, and in computing facilities close to the user ('edge computing'). European Commission (2020b).

[24] European Commission (2020b).

complying with European values.[25] Further, in order to boost technological innovation, the EC intends to promote data pools[26] enabling Big Data analytics and machine learning, in a manner compliant with data protection legislation and competition law, allowing the emergence of data-driven ecosystems. In order to facilitate the establishment of data pools, the EC will update of the Horizontal Co-operation Guidelines to provide more guidance to stakeholders on the compliance of data sharing and pooling arrangements with EU competition law.

Data sharing needs to be facilitated as much as possible, both for public sector information (government-to-business—G2B—Open Data Directive)[27] and business-to-business (B2B) relationships. G2B and B2B data sharing tools would be enshrined in the forthcoming (expected in 2022) EU Data Act. In the Data Act the EC will explore the viability of new tools to support individuals in enforcing their rights regarding the use of the data they generate. This could be supported by enhancing the portability right for individuals under Article 20 of the GDPR, giving them more control over who can access and use machine-generated data, for example through stricter requirements on interfaces for real-time data access and making machine-readable formats compulsory for data from certain products and services, e.g. data coming from smart home appliances or wearables. In addition, rules for providers of personal data apps or novel data intermediaries such as providers of personal data spaces could be considered, guaranteeing their role as a neutral broker.

The right to data portability under Article 20 of the GDPR, despite being a potential trigger for competition, is designed to enable switching of service providers rather than enabling data reuse in digital ecosystems. This right has practical limitations, thus, the EC worries that consumers of IoT digital services might still suffer from lock-in effects as well as unfair practices and discrimination.

In order to implement these policies, a cross-sectoral governance framework for data access and use will be needed. A number of decisions and measures will be implemented under the umbrella of an enabling

---

[25] European Commission (2020b).

[26] Data pools would act as a one-stop-shop allowing entities interested in having access to those data to interact just with a single administrator. Companies could send their data to a platform and get back aggregate data with no indication of which company it comes from.

[27] Directive (EU) 2019/1024 on open data and the re-use of public sector information.

legislative framework for the governance of common European data spaces. First, this would include a mechanism to prioritise standardisation activities aimed at delivering harmonised description and overview of datasets, data objects and identifiers to foster data interoperability (i.e. their usability at a technical level) between sectors and, where relevant, within sectors. Second, decisions as to which kinds of data can be used under the GDPR legal framework would be encouraged in order to increase legal certainty.

Investments in capabilities and infrastructures for hosting, processing and using data interoperability are going to be incentivised. In the period 2021–2027, the Commission will invest in a High Impact Project on Common European data spaces and federated cloud infrastructures. The project will fund infrastructures, data-sharing tools, architectures and governance mechanisms for thriving data-sharing and Artificial Intelligence ecosystems, in strategic economic sectors and domains of public interest (mobility data, health data, energy data, financial data, agriculture data, public administration data).[28]

Within the mentioned data strategy, the European Commission proposed a Data Governance Act (DGA), as an important milestone to boost a data-driven economy in Europe.[29]

The DGA covers three distinct elements.

First, for data held by public bodies, it enables the possibility to tap into those data that are currently not shared because of their sensitivity. In short, those data are sensitive because they concern someone's rights. Those rights could for instance deal with Intellectual Property, or commercial confidentiality. With these new rules, such data can be made available for reuse because their level of legitimate protection will be maintained, even if they travel to other countries.

Second, in order to facilitate voluntary data sharing while preserving control over the data from companies and individuals, principles for trustworthy intermediaries are provided. Several caveats will ensure this trust. First, intermediaries are required to notify the competent public authority of their intention to provide data-sharing services. They will ensure the protection of sensitive and confidential data. And they will have to comply with strict requirements to ensure their neutrality. In practice, this means

---

[28] European Commission (2020b).

[29] European Commission (2020c).

that data intermediaries will function as a neutral third party that connect data holders and data users. The framework offers an alternative model to the current data-handling practices offered by Big Tech platforms. Public bodies and companies will only be ready to share data if they are certain that their data will not be used by data sharing service providers for any other purposes than the ones they have mutually agreed to. This is all about providing a safe environment for those willing to share data.

The third element of the DGA is that these principles also apply to individuals whenever we wish to share our own personal data or donate them to serve the general interest. For instance, people suffering from rare diseases may voluntarily share the results of their medical tests to be used to improve treatments for those diseases. New so-called personal data spaces will ensure that people can keep control over their own data. The personal data spaces also ensure that they are only used for purposes agreed to, as in the above example for medical research.

This new regulation will therefore provide a governance framework that will ensure that data can be made available voluntarily by data holders and support common European data spaces. It will allow businesses, small and big, to benefit from an enhanced and easier access to data and from reduction in both costs and time in acquiring data.

6.3 THE DIGITAL MARKET ACT PROPOSAL: TOWARD A NE[X]T NEUTRALITY

The genesis of the Digital Markets Act (DMA), proposed in December 2020 by the Eu Commission,[30] is the result of the ongoing debate, described in Sect. 6.1, about if and how to tackle big platforms' economic and market power. The preliminary policy outcome somehow builds on the definitions and extend the scope of the concepts underlying the existing P2B regulation,[31] which regulates some of the relationships between online platforms and their business users (Sect. 4.3), extending the rationales and scope to end-users. Indeed, also following the policy indications from its public report, the EU Commission eventually abandoned a possible antitrust law reform, and proposed a

---

[30] European Commission (2020d) Proposal for a Regulation on contestable and fair markets in the digital sector (Digital Markets Act, DMA), COM (2020) 842 final.

[31] Regulation (EU) 2019/1150 on promoting fairness and transparency of business users of online intermediation services (P2B Regulation).

pro-competitive ex-ante regulatory regime aimed at facilitating market contestability and a fairer platform environment, rooting its legal base in Article 114 of the Treaty.[32]

The political debate on the DMA is currently ongoing before the EU Parliament and EU Council, therefore its final version could be subject to substantial amendments. Nevertheless, the fixed starting point of EU policy makers for the DMA is twofold: (a) competition law is not sufficient to address in an effective way the comprehensive lack of contestability and unfair practices that some providers of core platform services may generate; and (b) it is necessary an intervention at EU level, according to the EU principle of subsidiarity (Article 5 TFEU), in order to create harmonised rules for very large digital platforms consistently applied across all EU member states.

In light of the EU proportionality principle (the other side of the coin in Article 5 TFEU), the DMA's regulatory measures are expressly limited to core platform services (CPSs) defined as (i) online interme-diation services, (ii) online search engines, (iii) social networking, (iv) video-sharing platform services, (v) number-independent interpersonal electronic communication services, (vi) operating systems, (vii) cloud services, and (viii) advertising services (additional digital services may be added to the list). However, pursuant to Article 17(a) of the proposed DMA, new services may be added as a result of a market investigation.

Differently from competition law remedies, imposition of regulatory obligations under the DMA proposal is not dependent on a scrutiny of unilateral conducts held by firms with a (standard) dominant position in distinct relevant markets. The DMA establishes an ex-ante regula-tory framework where the necessary and sufficient precondition for being subject to regulation is to be a "gatekeeper" of a core platform service, in other words, a company providing one (or more) CPS and meeting three overarching criteria that qualify as a gatekeeper: (i) having a signifi-cant impact on the internal market; (ii) operating a core platform service which is an important gateway for business users to reach end users; (iii) enjoying an entrenched and durable position in its operations.[33] These

---

[32] That is the standard harmonisation procedure to establish the EU internal market, and which is the legal base of many sector-specific legislation, as the European Electronic Communications Code (EECC) Directive (EU) 2018/1972.

[33] Criterion (i) is presumed if the company provides a core platform service in at least three Member States and has annual revenues in the EU of at least 6.5 billion euros over

criteria have been seen as probably over-inclusive and for this reason it has been proposed the introduction of a fourth criteria consisting of the "orchestration of an ecosystem",[34] which would be very much coherent with the fact that gatekeeper's economic power is very often based on clusters and conglomerates, characterised by interdependent economic activities having an impact on the same set of users—as described with regards to platforms' envelopment strategies (Sect. 5.1).

The DMA proposal contains a long list of detailed ex-ante regulatory obligations imposed on designated gatekeepers. Two of them are crucial procedural obligation, imposing specific information duties. In particular, gatekeepers must notify to the EC (a) any plan of concentration with other gatekeepers, CPS providers, or other company active in the digital ecosystem, and (b) methods for profiling consumers that gatekeeper apply in CPS, after a scrutiny by an independent audit. As for the former obligation, this try to address one of the most critical aspect of the antitrust enforcement in digital markets, i.e., merger and acquisition control (Sect. 5.1 and Box 5.1). The latter notification aims to tackle the lack of information that public bodies have about platforms' internal functioning, which has been one of the impediments to develop a full and effective public regulatory capacity (Sects. 1.1 and 4.1). The DMA's substantive obligations are 18 and discipline four main areas of concerns: (a) use of and access to data; (b) interoperability; (c) business users' interactions with gatekeepers and end-users; and (d) end-users empowerment. Some of them, under Article 5, are to be executed without further specification, whereas some others, under Article 6, are "susceptible of being further specified" following a "regulatory dialogue" between the gatekeeper and the EU Commission. All of them are directly-applicable, as the DMA consider those behaviours as "particularly unfair or harmful", without any need of further analysis or case-by-case assessment. This setting, of course, scores very high in terms of process speeding, which is one of the DMA's objective, compared to competition law enforcement or to a possible principle-based ex-ante

---

the last three financial years, or if its average market was at least 65 billion euros over the last financial year. Criteria (ii) and (iii) are presumed to be met when the platform has monthly more than 45 million active end-users in the EU and more than 10,000 yearly active business users established in the EU in the last financial year.

[34] De Streel et al. (2021).

regulation (where specific obligations, consistent with principles in legislation, are imposed by regulators after a market analysis). However, not by chance principle-based regulation is usually adopted in complex and dynamic market context, where there trade-offs between certainty and flexibility. In other words a principle-based regulation is usually necessary where there are trade-offs between reducing enforcement costs (efficient **regulatory output**) and the overall welfare in the markets (efficient **regulatory outcome**). A framework of directly applicable obligations, such as those envisaged by the DMA, would likely tend to somehow sacrifice efficiency in the regulatory outcome, i.e., the overall effect on welfare, in order to facilitate an effective regulatory output.

Under a substantive point of view, as happened for regulatory frameworks adopted in other industries (even if CPSs are not an "industry" or a sector), i.e., for the electronic communications sector, most of the obligations defined in the ex-ante pro-competitive regulatory framework are the result of a "codification" of existing competition case-law and claims, in order to clearly pursue a competition promotion objective.

As happens in those sectors disciplined by a pro-competitive regulation, CPSs' gatekeepers will be subject to the new regulatory rules as well as competition law prohibitions, which will work as complements, just because competition law has been considered insufficient to address—or to effectively address—those practices in those market context.[35] This setting enlarges the scope of competition policy for digital markets, comprising now both competition law and pro-competitive regulation. Their interplay in digital markets is absolutely consistent with the established EU case-law (e.g., the Deutsche Telekom case in 2010), and above all with the existing hierarchical relationship between EU sources of law. As a matter of fact, competition law is enshrined in the Treaty, which is primary law, whereas regulatory acts are secondary law. Therefore, the DMA could in no case have the legal force to limit the application of article 101 and 102 TFEU: indeed it expressly aims to complement the enforcement of competition law and will applied without prejudice to Articles 101 and 102 TFEU.[36]

---

[35] Manganelli and Nicita (2020, section 3) regarding the electronic communications sector. As well as, Chirico (2021), specifically about the DMA.

[36] Recitals 5 and 9 DMA.

Indeed, DMA's objectives are convergent to competition law's ones, and stand within the realm of competition policy. As a matter of fact, two different public actions, and their outcomes, can be reasonably equated to services or goods that satisfy a specific public interest, or better "a public need", set as an objective by the law. In these terms, those activities, like all goods, can theoretically be independent or be characterised by a certain level of complementarity or substitutability to satisfy that need (under which their composition and interplay are evaluated). In other words, if competition law and DMA's platforms' regulation have a complementarity relationship, they work as complements in order to pursue a common (or greatly similar) objective.

On the contrary, the proposed regulation explicitly states that the DMA pursues an objective that is "different from that of protecting undistorted competition on any given market, as defined in competition law terms", which is to ensure that markets where gatekeepers are present are and remain contestable and fair, "independently from the actual, likely or presumed effects of the conduct of a given gatekeeper".[37]

As a matter of fact, neither the different legal basis, nor the different enforcement tools and principles, implies that the DMA protects a legal interest that is different from that protected by EU competition law: "both protect fair and undistorted competition but not (necessarily) as defined in competition law terms".[38] EU competition law and the DMA essentially share the same aims, although the latter should be read as an effort to recalibrate the goals of EU competition policy: away from the protection of consumer welfare, back towards a protection of competition as a process.

Under DMA's Article 10(2), a behaviour is unfair or has the effect to limit the CPSs' contestability if: (a) there is an imbalance of rights and obligations on business users and the gatekeeper is obtaining an advantage from business users that is disproportionate to the service provided by the gatekeeper to business users; or (b) the contestability of markets is weakened as a consequence of such a practice engaged in by gatekeepers.

These definitions are quite vague, however seem to fall within the scope of competition policy. Market contestability is obviously a goal for competition policy. Also fairness, as used in the DMA, does not

---

[37] Recital 10 DMA.

[38] Schweitzer (2021).

imply a redistributive action, yet a counterbalancing of bargaining and market power of 'dominant' players, which is a typical objective of pro-competitive regulation. Furthermore, DMA uses those terms, i.e., fairness and contestability, nearly exclusively together, as a single concept. Indeed, there is no clear allocation of each remedy to a specific objective, while Article 7 clearly states that "the measures implemented by the gatekeeper to ensure compliance with the obligations laid down in Articles 5 and 6 shall be effective in achieving the objective of the relevant obligation".[39] In any case, especially as embodied by the DMA's prescriptions, "both these objectives are best understood as part and parcel of competition policy".[40]

The policy maker's intention is to build a set of obligations[41] having a cumulative pro-competitive impact on digital markets whose specific market failures are addressed in a systematic way.[42] This implies that further specifications of obligations at Article 6, and also compliance with Article 5, should be based on the specific market failure that each obligation aims to address.

Indeed, "one of the main challenges in the implementation of the DMA is how to separate the positive efficiency and welfare gains that plat-form generate through (data-driven) network effects from negative anti-competitive and welfare-reducing platforms' behaviours. Pro-competitive remedies should not undermine the efficiency gains of platforms".[43]

In other words, obligations aimed to pursue contestability and fairness should be oriented to remedy a specific market failure and should not be—detrimental for the (static and dynamic allocative) efficiency of the market.

The relationship between efficiency (productive and allocative), on one side, and fairness (i.e., redistributive considerations), on the other side, should be at the core of any ex-ante pro-competitive regulatory

---

[39] De Streel et al. (2021).

[40] Larouche and de Streel (2021).

[41] Complementary between each other, on one side, and complementary to competition law enforcement, on the other side. This approach goes beyond what could be achieved under Article 102 TFEU which can just address, retrospectively, certain forms of envelopment that the dominant firm has used.

[42] Monti (2021).

[43] Cabral et al. (2021).

framework for digital platforms, at least as far as asymmetric regulation is concerned. When obligations are not imposed to all market players but only to a subset of them, as in the DMA, because of their characteristics and thus the effect that their behaviours could create, it seems necessary to actually perform an analysis of the actual impact in the market. Indeed, an effect-based regulation of digital platforms should aim to strike a balance between (i) the static and dynamic market value of information "created" and services provided by digital platforms and (ii) fairness vis-à-vis business users, potential competitors, and final consumers. This could be done, as some commentators have proposed, by (a) introducing some kind of efficiency and proportionality assessment, either as a defence—however, this would contravene the Commission's objective to speed-up the enforcement process—, or (b) carrying out a preliminary thorough cost-benefit analysis aimed to select, and consequently include in the DMA, only those obligations having an overall welfare-enhancing effect, and not extending to all gatekeeper antitrust case-law specific to one (some) of them. An intermediate, more balanced, solution could be to differentiate remedies according to the different digital markets (not strictly identified as relevant market for competition law purposes), the nature and modes of the gatekeeping power, and (maybe, considering the tiny number of gatekeepers) the gatekeeper platform itself.

This is crucial: while all incumbent operators in a pro-competitively regulated sector (such as telecom markets) are very similar in terms of business models and how they exercise their market and bargaining power, on the contrary, a complete harmonisation of ex-ante remedies across the different core platform services could turn out to be quite problematic—just because digital markets are not a sector.

Even considering only GAFAM, they all have very different features (see Sect. 5.1). Although all of them would likely fit the core platform services definition and the gatekeeper qualitative and quantitative thresholds, they have different business models, source of revenues, market integration (envelopment) strategies, strategy on use of data, interoperability and standardisation approach. Therefore, the way in which gatekeeping power is exerted varies across platforms' business models and CPS, requiring differentiated regulatory remedies.[44]

---

[44] Caffarra and Scott Morton (2021).

As mere examples, not all CPSs are two-sided platforms performing intermediary functions: some CPSs are single-sided, as it is the case for number-independent interpersonal communication services as well as cloud computing services.[45] Furthermore, different CPSs are characterised by a different importance of scale on the supply side, and on the demand side (network externalities), and data, so the concentration drivers are very heterogeneous.[46]

Against this differentiation, in the current version of the DMA proposal, remedies' flexibility is formally limited only to a proportionality principle for obligations to be further specified (Article 6). As emphasised,[47] this inflexibility risks to undermine rules effectiveness and the achievement of the framework's objectives, possibly creating unintended consequences. A more market-specific approach would probably much better fit the diverse and dynamic features of digital platforms. That is the approach adopted in the UK, where ex-ante regulatory obligations for each online platform having a "strategic market status"[48] will be designed by a specific code of conducts, defined by a Digital Markets Unit (set up within the CMA) in cooperation with the designated company (co-regulation). Furthermore, this limited flexibility in the DMA may have an impact on the capacity of rules to adapt to market changes: a feature that is extremely relevant in digital markets. Actually, the proposed regulation provides for the possibility for the EC to update the list of obligations at Article 5 and 6, adding new types of harmful practices or removing obsolete ones, by issuing a delegated act. However, in case of new unfair or anti-competitive behaviours, the EC has always the choice to apply competition law: if a new undesirable behaviour is carried out by a single gatekeeper and it is specific to that gatekeeper, then opening an antitrust case would probably be preferable. Instead, in front of a general (actual

---

[45] De Streel et al. (2021). Moreover, those two services are already regulated by EU law, and those rules should be coordinated: number-independent interpersonal communication services are covered by the EECC and subject to transparency and interoperability obligations: Article 61 (2) EECC; whereas cloud services are covered by the Free Flow of Data Regulation which encourages codes of conducts to facilitate the porting of data and the switching between cloud providers: Article 6 Regulation 2018/1807 on a framework for the free flow of non-personal data in the European Union.

[46] Ducci (2020).

[47] Caffarra and Scott Morton (2021).

[48] Substantial and entrenched market power and strategic position.

or potential) conduct, regulation is better suited to discipline all market players. This evaluation, however, should also be at the basis of the development of the current DMA's obligations, avoiding a generalised (to all gatekeepers) application of detailed rules designed on a specific case/platform.

In this regard, few interesting amendment proposals have been put forward: (a) to condition rules on identified business models, thus creating different set of rules for each category[49]; (b) to create not only (two different) black lists, yet also a grey list of gatekeepers' behaviours, indicating those conducts that are merely presumed to be "unfair and against contestability" and gatekeepers have to the possibility to demonstrate a fair and pro-competitive nature and effect[50]; and (c) increasing flexibility and enforcement discretion by (c_i) giving gatekeepers the possibility to request an 'exemption decision' from the Commission under specific circumstance,[51] and (c_{ii}) including an additional comprehensive prohibition, formulated in a general principle-based manner,[52] as it happens, for example, for the Unfair Commercial Practice Directive (Sect. 4.3). Of course any enforcement flexibility should be based onto a centralised institutional setting, in order to avoid problematic fragmentation of rules and their application at national level. Indeed, under an institutional viewpoint, the DMA is based on a strong centralisation, as solely the EU commission is empowered to apply those rules. This setting is justified by the global nature of gatekeepers and their disruptive impact onto markets. It is true that other EU pro-competitive regulatory frameworks as well as competition law have decentralised enforcement settings. However, that institutional design is justified, as for regulation, by the national dimension/nature of regulated incumbents, and, as for competition law enforcement, by the fact that its "modernisation" in 2003 (i.e., empowerment of national competition authorities) took place only

---

[49] Caffarra and Scott Morton (2021).

[50] Cabral et al. (2021)

[51] For example, "if (a) the particular circumstances of the gatekeeper or the CPS mean that imposing that obligation would undermine rather than bolster contestability or fairness or (b) the cumulative effect of other obligations applied to a specific gatekeeper make the imposition of that specific obligation unnecessary or disproportionate for achieving the objectives of contestability or fairness".

[52] Larouche and de Streel (2021).

after decades of centralised antitrust enforcement by the Commission and EU courts, which built a consolidated core case-law.

Finally, it seems necessary to enhance coordination between DMA and other pieces of the digital ecosystem legislative framework, notably, all the rules related to data. As described in Sect. 5, the collection and exchange of data, on the one side, and the management and valorisation, on the other side, are at the core of platform economy and platforms' economic (i.e., gatekeeping) power. The proposed DMA regulation supplements the data protection legislation, imposing transparency obligations and prohibitions of consumers' cross-profiling, which will contribute to a better application of an enhanced level of protection in the GDPR. Moreover, DMA Article 6(1)(h) and (i) define rights to data portability, as also previously done by Article 20 of the GDPR, as an individual right for a single user to *"have the personal data transmitted directly from one controller to another, where technically feasible"*. This could contribute to discipline digital giants, giving gatekeepers' competitors the possibility to have the same information and create a competitive level playing field ('contestability objective').

Indeed, data portability may reduce exit costs—that is, the opportunity cost to switch platforms—and, at the same time, it may allow new entrants to access the data of users, so that information and personalised services can be provided. However, per se, data portability would most likely have a limited pro-competitive impact. As a matter of fact, users' data portability is intrinsically linked with switching, therefore—where switching costs are extremely large and constitutes an obstacle to users' mobility, as it is the case for big tech because of pervasive network externalities—data portability likely turns out to be mostly ineffective.

In other words, data portability addresses the competitive problem creating a formal obligation on the supply side, yet users are not, in fact, empowered to exercise the correlated data portability right, since network externalities may constitute an insurmountable switching and exit cost. By the way, this is what would happen also in the telecom markets, if liberalisation, i.e., abolition of exclusive and special monopoly rights, would have not been coupled with a pro-competitive regulatory framework aimed to counterbalance the former monopolists' substantive power.[53] Indeed, a primary supply-side obligation in telecom markets refers to networks'

---

[53] Manganelli and Nicita (2020).

interconnection, aimed to internalise networks externalities that would otherwise represent a huge switching cost for consumer and entry barrier for smaller/new companies. This regulatory remedy would correspond *mutatis mutandis* to an extensive interoperability obligation imposed on digital platforms.

As a matter of facts, within the telecom framework, it is also foreseen an interoperability obligation that National regulators (jointly with EU Commission) may impose to those number-independent interpersonal communications services (provided by OTTs)[54] that would reach a significant level of coverage and user uptake, in those circumstances where end-to-end connectivity between end-users could be endangered.[55] Also the DMA proposal, under Article 6(1)(f), features an interoperability obligation to be further specified, covering business users' and ancillary services. Supply-side interoperability obligations might be somehow extended in specific circumstances, maintaining proportionality features, but should be tailored on the specific platform service and use-case, carefully considering technical feasibility, economic rationale, and all potential unintended side-effects.[56]

This approach, rather than an access obligation to data,[57] would be much more consistent with the fact (Sects. 5.2 and 5.3) that platforms' dominance, prominence or significant power in the market does not originate from an essential facility, but essentially from network externalities combined with privatisation of market information and the absence of a data market. Indeed, interoperability and data portability would partially

---

[54] Number Independent CS are those where the number is only the user's identification and not assigned and used for routing operations, e.g., provided by the OTTs (e.g., Skype, WhatsApp). Those are subject to a light-touch regulation, e.g., OTTs are explicitly exempted from the general authorisation regime, as they do not benefit from the use of public numbering resources.

[55] Article 61 (2) c EECC.

[56] According to Larouche and de streel (2021), "DMA should go further than it does in imposing obligations for gatekeepers to ensure interconnection and interoperability with competing CPS providers".

[57] As mentioned in the previous section, however, mandating access to data do not seem to be able to completely tackle the competitive problems. First of all, it is not data, but the information extrapolated from data by algorithms which give Big Techs such competitive advantage and allows them to become the "market". Algorithms' efficiency, i.e., their ability to extract relevant information from data, has been progressively enhanced by the availability of an increasing amount of refined data. So, it is in theory possible to transfer data, but not the algorithm efficiency that has built data.

recreate a context of public—or better collective/common—information within the market and its exchanges.

An additional crucial complement to this approach should look at the demand of platform services, or, better, at the supply-side of data, by defining data property rights. This would represent a substantive action for data transferability, which could be applied horizontally to all digital markets, making digital data transaction explicit and thus creating the necessary condition for an effective data market to emerge. A data market would allow new platforms to access user data to such an extent to develop efficient entry dynamics and sustainable competition. Moreover, this would allow to remedy an evident unfair outcome, as there is no fair distribution and participation of users in profits and value generated by digital data transactions ('fairness objective'). Indeed, "platform economy leads to unfair outcomes where users are not rewarded for their contribution to the success of the platform and regulation should aim at correcting this distortion".[58]

As previously highlighted, absent interoperability obligations, in order to overcome network effects, a minimum number of relevant users or a minimum scale of overall users must transfer their data to a new platform. This requires a costly and difficult coordination activity of users for the management of a collective switching from an incumbent platform (or even just a collective bargaining regarding a possible switching, that is what is relevant to exert an effective competitive pressure). This opens the way for new third-party data intermediary and/or aggregators, which on behalf of the users could coordinate the (potential) switching to an alternative platform.

In this regard, as mentioned in Sect. 6.2, another EU regulation proposal, i.e., the Data Governance Act (DGA), is focusing on data sharing services and data intermediaries, in order to, *inter alia*, "*sharing of data among businesses, against remuneration in any form*", and "*allowing personal data to be used with the help of a 'personal data-sharing intermediary', designed to help individuals exercise their rights under the GDPR*".

These new data market actors would be third-party operators, i.e., vertically non-integrated. These intermediaries could aggregate several data users, counterbalancing platforms' bargaining power. They can then

---

[58] Crawford et al. (2021). Also De Michelis di Slonghello and Bolognini (2018).

support the valorisation of data implicitly exchanged by users and monetise that data by either (a) negotiate on their behalf to obtain a better deal vis-à-vis the platforms, or (b) comparing different data rewarding conditions in different platforms and guide the consumers' choice for a collective switching (like a digital comparison tool). In this regard, the DGA focuses on data sharing services and data intermediaries, in order facilitate data sharing and circulation, in respect of the GDPR, whereas a much deeper and relevant effect could be the promotion of competitive pressure on the demand-side, through a specific coordination with the DMA.

However, in order to follow this competitive enhancing path, users must have well-defined data property rights to the control and clearly allocate their possible uses, resulting from clear negotiations, and allow specific uses and rights to the intermediaries. So, the most effective approach would be on the consumer side, defining transferability obligations on the platforms supply side (data portability) and well-defined right on the demand side of services (or better the data supply side) (see Sect. 5.3).

In this sense, a fair and contestable digital ecosystem is a place where "net neutrality" principles are applied also to platform- user (or business user) relationship. Indeed, digital fairness and contestability is a call for future-proof *neutral networks*, both physical and virtual, in each and every level of the digital ecosystem. Here, the idea of *ne[x]t neutrality*[59] that is an evolution of the net neutrality concept (Sect. 4.2), implemented by rules aimed to cover all possible contexts of opacity and unfair discrimination in each of the relationships constituting the digital transaction—i.e., among Internet Access Providers, Content Application Providers, Platforms, Business Users, End-Users. A ne[x]t neutrality approach should be applied broadly to all ecosystem's actors, yet identifying economic and business specificities and distinguishing relations of substitutability and complementarity. Ne[x]t neutrality rules and implementation are therefore a form of pro-competitive regulation, as in the combination of some provisions and rationales proposed by the DMA and the DGA, including the key role played in the market by empowered consumers.

Focusing on the systemic nature of digital transactions leads to interpreting all piece of regulation of digital markets as a means to find a

---

[59] Manganelli and Nicita (2020, section 8.4).

balance of power in the digital market society, where private rules set by platforms (Sect. 4.1) must be disciplined by regulatory measures, which, in turn, must be declined, in strength, scope, and flexibility, depending on the actual market structure, complementary-substitutability of relationships, business models, and type and intensity of gatekeeping power.

REFERENCES

AGCM, AGCOM, GPDP. (2019). *Big Data.*
Australian Competition and Consumer Commission, ACCC. (2019). *Digital platforms inquiry* (pp. 44–55).
Bourreau, M., & de Streel, A. (2019). *Digital conglomerates and EU competition policy.* CERRE Policy Paper.
Cabral, L., Haucap, J., Parker, G., Petropoulos, G., Valletti, T., & Van Alstyne M. (2021). *The EU Digital Markets Act.* JRC Report.
Caffarra, C., & Scott Morton, F. (2021). *How will the digital markets act regulate big tech?* ProMarket.
Chirico, F. (2021). Digital markets act: A regulatory perspective. *Journal of European Competition Law & Practice, 12,* 7.
CMA. (2019). *Market study on online platforms and digital advertising—Interim report of the UK competition and markets authority.*
Colangelo, G. (2020). *Evaluating the case for regulation of digital platforms.* The Global Antitrust Institute Report on the Digital Economy.
Crawford, G., Crémer, J., Dinielli, D., Fletcher, A., Heidhues, P., Schnitzer, M., Scott Morton, F., & Seim, K. (2021). *Fairness and contestability in the Digital Markets Act* (Discussion Paper No. 3). Yale Digital Regulation Project, Policy.
Crémer, J., de Montjoye, Y.-A., & Schweitzer, H. (2019). *Competition policy for the digital era.* EU Commission.
De Michelis di Slonghello, I., & Bolognini, L. (2018). *An introduction to the right to monetize (RTM).* Mimeo.
De Streel, A., Feasey, R., Kramer, J., & Monti, G. (2021). *Making the Digital Markets Act more resilient and effective.* CERRE paper.
Ducci, F. (2020). *Natural monopolies in digital platform markets.* Cambridge University Press.
European Commission. (2016). *Connectivity for a competitive digital single market towards a European gigabit society.* COM/2016/0587 final.
European Commission. (2020a). Communication "Shaping Europe's digital future".
European Commission. (2020b). Communication EU data strategy.

European Commission. (2020c). *Proposal for a regulation of the European Parliament and of the council on European data governance* (Data Governance Act). COM/2020/767 final.

European Commission. (2020d). *Proposal for a Regulation on contestable and fair markets in the digital sector* (Digital Markets Act), COM/2020/ 842 final.

European Commission. (2021). Communication "Digital compass 2030—The European way for the digital decade".

Furman J., Coyle, D., Fletcher A., Marsden, P., & McAuley, D. (2019). *Unlocking digital competition.* British Digital Competition Expert Panel.

Larouche, P., & de Streel, A. (2021). The European Digital Markets Act: A revolution grounded on traditions. *Journal of European Competition Law & Practice, 12*(7), 561–575.

Manganelli, A., & Nicita, A. (2020). *The governance of telecom markets.* Palgrave MacMillan.

Monti, G. (2021) *The Digital Markets Act. Institutional design and suggestions for improvement* (TILEC Discussion Paper No. 4).

Schallbruch, M., Schweitzer H., & Wambach A. (2019). *A new competition framework for the digital economy.* German Commission 'Competition Law 4.0'

Schweitzer, H. (2021) *The art to make gatekeeper positions contestable and the challenge to know what is fair: A discussion of the Digital Markets Act proposal.* Mimeo.

Schweitzer, H., Haucap, H., Kerber, K., & Welker, W. (2018). *Modernisation of abuse control for companies with a dominant market position* (pp. 59–78).

Stigler Committee for the Study of Digital Platforms. (2019). *Market structure and antitrust subcommittee.* University of Chicago.

Stucke, M., & Grunes, A. (2016). *Big data and competition policy.* Oxford University Press.

Tirole, J. J. (2020). *Competition and the industrial challenge for the digital age.* Mimeo.

CHAPTER 7

Regulating Platforms' Digital Services: Speech and Reach

Abstract The spread of online platforms has resulted in a transformation of marketplaces and information systems, where algorithms are used to provide a wide range of digital services, e.g., to communicate, buy goods or access/provide online information. This process has raised the demand for a digital space where users' fundamental rights are protected, and businesses can enjoy a level playing field. One of the main concern relates to how algorithmic efficiency can impact pluralism. Beside the benefits of digital transformation, the trade and exchange of illegal and harmful content, as well as the creation of biased sources of information, and the risk of limited free choice or limited expression have called for a regulatory intervention. The European Commission has launched a proposal for a new regulation, the Digital Services Act, aimed to set rules for a safe, predictable and trusted online platform's environment, where digital fundamental rights are protected. A primary objective is to address disinformation issues by introducing transparency and accountability duties on digital intermediaries and platforms, ultimately to preserve the EU core democratic values.

Keywords On-line information system · Pluralism 2.0 · Disinformation · Digital Service Act

A. Manganelli and A. Nicita, *Regulating Digital Markets*, Palgrave Studies in Institutions, Economics and Law, https://doi.org/10.1007/978-3-030-89388-0_7

7.1   Public Policy for Digital Services: From "Neutrality" to "Moderation"

Beside Big Tech's 'economic' power across several intermediated markets (and markets' sides), other important issues have emerged regarding the vast array of digital services, especially for those digital intermediaries and CPS providers delivering 'content and information', such as search engines (e.g., Google, Yahoo!, Bing, etc.), video-sharing platforms (e.g., YouTube, Netflix etc.), social networks (e.g., Twitter, Facebook, Instagram, etc.), channels in cloud-based instant messaging system (e.g., Telegram), online shopping platforms (i.e., Amazon, eBay, etc.) and so on.

One of the core issues, originally raised in the policy debate, regarded online platforms' liability over illegal content uploaded or downloaded by users, mainly represented by copyright infringements, violation of privacy, child sexual abuse material, terrorist content, and hate speech, in countries having legislations aimed at protecting citizens and right holders against these kinds of illegal contents.

All the above cases refer to the impact of digital services on users' rights, and the general right to have a safe online environment. These represents crucial aspects of the Digital Fundamental and Constitutional Rights (see Sect. 4.2).

Consumers ability to have a free informed choices on the selection of content and information uploads and downloads, or on the choice to opt out from a specific platform/market frame, is affected by the economic mechanisms and commercial strategies at the base of platform economy (as described in Sects. 5.2 and 5.3), that is: (a) the establishment of a business model based on implicit exchange between free services and data, in a multi-sided market context, and (b) the ability of reaching efficient outcomes similar to a perfect competition context, by internalising and exploiting information about preferences and willingness to pay of each customer. According to the Open public consultation on a New Competition Tool, launched by the European Commission, 60% of respondents say that consumers don't have sufficient choices and alternatives regarding online platforms. This puzzling answer seems raising a paradox: how it is possible that the web, that allow full access to a wide range of information and contents, could actually be reducing consumers' choices? The answer is quite complex. On the one side, digital platforms reduce consumers' transaction costs by governing and simplifying information overload;

on the other side, platforms increase consumers' dependence from the algorithmic filter and consumers' exposure towards micro-targeting advertisement. This is particularly true for those transactions affected by unfair practices and lack of transparency. Moreover, with a low degree of service interoperability, platforms users cannot fully compare choices available, as well as their prices. Increased costs to switch platforms certainly affect users' possibility to compare the set of choices available to them (both in terms of access to contents and services and of data profiling). Thanks to their role of intermediaries in multi-sided markets, digital platforms may eventually impose unfair take-it-or-leave-it conditions on both their business users and consumers, reducing the choices actually available in the market. Moreover, according to the 2018 Eurobarometer survey, 61% of EU citizens say they have come across illegal content online, and 65% say they think the Internet is not safe to be used. Among new remedies requested by consumers to improve these situations, there are: (a) increased transparency over the rules adopted for content moderation; (b) greater information about advertising and targeted ads in order to understand who sponsored the ad, and how and why it targets a specific user; (c) clearer information on why a given content is recommended to users; (d) users' right to opt-out from content recommendations based on profiling; (e) better access to data for authorities and researchers in order to better understand virality online and its impact with a view to lower societal risks. Many digital platforms then decided to implement self-regulation policies (codes of conduct), also including (some of) the above remedies, in order to contrast illegal contents. Nevertheless, much has still to be done to allow an easy and clear reporting of illegal content, goods or services on online platforms, as well as to impose transparency on platforms' implementation of their codes of conduct.

As seen in Sect. 6.1, these concerns call for a regulatory action much closer to the legacy of ex-ante pro-competitive regulation and consumer protection, rather than to ex-post antitrust interventions.

This is even more true considering users' choices for digital services, especially 'content and information', which affects, in turn, several relevant fundamental rights: freedom to speech (to produce and to receive information), freedom to reach (to reach and to be reached by a desired audience), freedom not to be informed[1] and not to be misinformed,[2] freedom to choose the degree of data-driven profiling, freedom to be subject to online micro targeting, freedom not to be harassed and so on.

The actual self-regulatory treatment of illegal and harmful online contents by digital platform, had origin in the so-called *Good Samaritan rule*, introduced in section 230 title 47 of the U.S. Code, enacted as part of the United States Communications Decency Act, in 1996. As described in the above Sect. 3.1 and following Sect. 7.5, a similar rule have been echoed few years later, in 2000, in the EU e-commerce directive and now to be amended by the EU Digital Service Act (DSA). The Good Samaritan rule provides a comprehensive immunity for digital platforms with respect to third-party content: immunity from liability for providers and users of an "interactive computer service" who publish information provided by third-party user (c.1) (similar to article 12 of the e-commerce Directive); and a "Good Samaritan" protection from civil liability for digital platforms decisions to remove or moderate third-party material, even when constitutionally protected (as free speech) (c.2) (similar to what the DSA will introduce in the EU digital legal system).

Section 230 has been interpreted as a necessary protection for digital intermediaries of third-party contents who are not "editors" of the contents such as traditional radio and TV broadcasters. At the same time, digital platforms had the right to introduce self-regulated moderation of contents hosted in the platform in order to keep a safe digital environment (including removal decisions), respecting their own terms of service.

To some extent, the two above immunity provisions show some internal tension. Indeed, on the one side, the first liability exemption (against third-party content) maintains a vision of digital platforms as a *neutral environment*, a sort of open public sphere of online discussion, where the platform acts as a *mere conduit* enabler, without playing any role as regards to the nature of the content delivered. However, on the other side, the option for platforms to moderate contents according to their terms of services, without being qualified as liable for that, envisages a policy that, at least in some respects, violates the above assumption of *mere conduit*, i.e. of platforms' neutrality over content delivery. Moreover, as outlined below, the rules and procedures governing upload and

---

[1] Sunstein (2020).

[2] Sunstein (2021).

download of online contents, as well as the selection of contents reached, are far from being "neutral", as they are actually decided by algorithmic profiling based on individual released data.

Thus section 230, and its internal contradiction, reflect the political and policy approach aimed at avoiding chilling effects and boosting digital platforms at their beginning, as a new complex information system needing some immunity to resist to legal challenges in courts.

On the other side, section 230 provisions do not protect content providers against the removal of illegal content at a federal level, such as in case of copyright infringement. In 2018, section 230 was amended by the Stop Enabling Sex Traffickers Act (FOSTA-SESTA).

In the following years, protections from section 230 have come under closer scrutiny and in May 2020 an Executive Order by US President Trump claimed that moderation policies by Big Techs went too far, alleging the emergence of "online censorship", and urging Congress, FTC and FCC to adopt measures to reform section 230, against the risk of platforms violating first amendment protection on free speech. The Order was announced on Twitter by Donald Trump, a few days before, as a response to Twitter's flagging as "disputed content" a previous message posted by Trump alleging fraudulent mail in ballots over the incoming presidential elections. After the Capitol Assault on 6 January 2021, Facebook,[3] and Twitter,[4] suspended Trump's account as a result of alleged serious and repeated violations of their terms of services—as rules governing the interaction within those specific legal orderings (Sect. 4.1).

Few weeks after, President Biden, while revoking the previous Trump's Executive Order, confirmed, amid the battle against misinformation concerning covid-19 and vaccines, the intention to revise section 230 in the near future. Biden's vision[5] seems, however, going in a different direction, towards increased strength in facing disinformation strategies and liabilities for illegal and harmful contents.

In this chapter we mainly focus on issues related to disinformation and the need to increase transparency and accountability in data managing and profiling, as well as in content moderation, by digital platforms. In order

[3] https://about.fb.com/news/2021/01/responding-to-the-violence-in-washington-dc/.

[4] https://blog.twitter.com/en_us/topics/company/2020/suspension.

[5] https://edition.cnn.com/2021/07/20/politics/white-house-section-230-facebook/index.html.

to fully understand the role of digital platforms in designing the online information space, it is important to investigate first how users' algorithmic profiling contributes to the selection of specific content, matching users' preferences and to the design of platforms' moderation policies.

7.2   ALGORITHMIC DESIGN AND CONTENT SELECTION

Algorithmic design is at the core of the functioning of online platforms' digital services as they affect both the nature of content selected and delivered to users and the way in which platforms adopt, monitor and enforce their moderation policies. It is the efficiency of algorithmic design that on the one side, captures the attention of users, by providing appealing information to them, and on the other allows micro targeting ads to reach their purposes.

As we have seen, the algorithmic mechanism that assures *efficient matching* between contents producers and seekers, on the one side, and platforms and advertisers, on the other side, is at the core of the digital transaction. Platforms' business models, however, also require users' "stickiness" or engagement, i.e. the platform's ability to capture users' attention, in terms of time spent over consuming platforms' contents. Typically, this outcome occurs through 'suggesting' related contents.

As these domains are shaped by algorithmic profiling design over "big data", the analysis of the design of digital services still refers to three different sides of the digital transaction:

i. the side of content seekers, whose freedom to choose contents is constrained by the particular selection 'suggested' by algorithms, according to the preferences revealed by users' digital footprint;
ii. the side of content producers whose freedom to reach content seekers is managed by the platforms' algorithms;
iii. the side of advertisers whose freedom to match contents producers and seekers is managed and monetised by the platforms' algorithms.

The spread of online platforms and, especially of social networks (included in the wider concept of the social media), has resulted in a shift from a vertically integrated model for "news", typically that of offline publishing where the publisher exercises control (directly or indirectly) over content selection, to a separation of the different "productive" stages. Online information is increasingly replacing the "news", as many citizen today get informed via the web, in general, and specifically via social networks. Online access to content changed the nature of the information selected by users and its access, allowing the same users to participate in the production and re-production of content and, thereby, reducing the role and room of intervention for intermediaries, such as traditional newspaper, radio, and TV editors. This phenomenon, as we have seen in previous chapters, dramatically enhanced the success of microtargeting and customised advertising, increasing value on the platform's side.

At the same time, on the information supply-side, the augmented availability of information sources has increased the so-called "external pluralism" (i.e., pluralism driven by competing information sources) and widened free speech, both in terms of freedom to inform others and freedom of getting informed by comparing competing alternative sources.

In this context, each user can create his own "broadcasting" or "newspaper" online (the *Daily Me* newspaper).[6] However, this enormous increase of information supply over the Internet, raised the 'information overload' issue: how to select "relevant" content from the ocean of decentralised information inputs?

It is here where the role of platforms' algorithms becomes decisive. In traditional media markets, reputation and brand loyalty of main newspapers, radio and TV networks act as selection mechanisms of the information suppliers, which are implicitly delegated by the audience/readers to select information and content. There, audience/readers selected competing contents, through their free choice over competing editorial outlets. In the web, this selection mechanism is mainly performed by platforms' algorithms: users' revealed data allow algorithmic profiling, so as to select the content with the highest probability of (having been) demand(ed) by each user. This means that platforms' users certainly make a free and informed choose, but within an information environment designed, tailored and selected on purpose by algorithms.

As too much information is experienced on the supply side, this algorithmic selective process reduces the time otherwise needed to assess potential contents, filter them, and ultimately select them. Thus, algorithms minimise transaction costs in the online information market. It

---

[6] Sunstein (2001, 2020).

is the *information overload* that render it efficient, and useful, the work done by algorithms.

According to Nobel Prize Winner Herbert Simon, "a wealth of information creates a poverty of attention and a need to allocate that attention efficiently among the overabundance of *information* sources that might consume it". Users' attention is a scarce resource, as it is the time users can and will spend in seeking information. A recent study showed how the competition in supplying information, in a situation of scarcity of attention, diminishes the knowledge of consumers.[7]

However, as mentioned, platforms algorithms perform also another task: once users connect to some 'selected' content, and further reveal their preferences, the algorithm also make "suggestions" over other contents which users might be interested in. This feature has to do with the other side of the digital transaction, i.e. with the microtargeted advertising, whose aim is to reach potential consumers.

This raise, in turn, the need to generate what has been defined "stickiness" or "engagement", i.e. the need for the platform (and its paying clients on the online advertising market side) to continue attracting the (scarce) attention of users (and the associated data that reveals their preferences).

As a consequence, algorithmic content selection becomes a complex, enduring, process whose ultimate aim is to maximise the time users spend within the platform and thus to maximize the value for the ad-side of the transaction.

This process is clearly far from being "neutral", both in the way information and data are collected and in the way contents are organised and proposed to users.

For example, Facebook's *newsfeed* was originally made up of the ranking and flows of news that the platform provides for its user on the website's homepage. It was the algorithm that was suggesting the news. A recent experiment, carried out in Argentina by the World Wide Web Foundation, demonstrated just how sensitive a social network's newsfeed is to the slight variations in users' online behaviours, and not only when ordering information selected, but also when defining what subset of information will be shown. The experiment involved creating a group of identical accounts: just a single feature was changed in only two of

---

[7] Persson (2018). As for the quotation: Simon (1971)

these, while the other accounts, the control group, remained unaltered. The single feature changed in these two accounts was only a *like* given by each of them respectively for a government representative and an opposition representative. Suddenly, the newsfeed segmented the world, selecting different news, different rankings and even omitting some news. In general, only a small part of the important news was shown, producing a polarised orientation. In short, a single *like* ended up changing the information landscape that the two hypothetical subjects received from the social network algorithm (https://webfoundation.org/2018/04/how-facebook-manages-your-information-diet-argentina-case-study/).

This high level of *sensitivity* to the content selected by the algorithm may generate a filter bubble,[8] referring to the personalised, and polarised virtual environment, characterised by poor permeability and high self-referencing, that algorithms build through the elaboration of each user's preferences and selections. In December 2018, Zoe Lofgren, a US Congress member, asked the CEO of Google, Sundar Pichai, during a hearing: "Why if you Google the word 'idiot' under images, a picture of Donald Trump comes up? Is it some little man sitting behind the curtains figuring out what to show the user?". Pichai explained that it's due to matching keywords from pages and then ranking them based on more than two hundred *signals* captured by the algorithms resulting from the huge amounts of information and millions of discussions on the web. A relevant case regarded the British protests organised during Trump's visit to the UK where the protestors launched a campaign to push to the top of the hits, Green Day's *American Idiot*, linking it to Trump's image.

An experimental study[9] has advanced an hypothesis about the existence of "a search engine manipulation effect", where ranking distortions can influence electors' choices, for example favouring the status quo.

As information seekers engaged in an information search journey, users end up at the first stop (*one-stop shop*) with the information package built in just a few clicks. And like all packaging made in a hurry, it contains only those things that are (believed to be) needed. But what users (believe to) need is often just what confirms already existing vision of the world. In selecting relevant information, users are actually attracted by contents that confirm their previous ideas, their starting convictions.

---

[8] A concept introduced by the American journalist Pariser.

[9] Epstein and Robertson (2015).

This is a cognitive distortion called *confirmation bias*. This *mental shortcut* is the second reason that reduces information search, along with information overload. In the online world, the content selection operated by search engine or social network algorithms acts as a self-enforcing and self-reinforcing device of confirmation bias. Algorithmic selection precisely suggests those contents that could probably interest users, based on their past choices patterns or also their friends' choices. On a similar vein, group experience (*groupthink*) among users with homogenous preferences reinforces users' beliefs and cognitive distortions, polarising them towards an even more extreme vision. In turn, polarisation is reinforced by "ignorance": according to, several empirical analyses how online content seekers tend to overestimate their actual knowledge and competences, a paradox known as the *Dunning-Kruger effect*. Many experiments reveal how the less we know about a subject, the more we stick to our convictions, distrusting those who question them, thus polarising our opinion. The existence of web-induced confirmation bias, polarisation and filter bubbles has been challenged by many empirical studies, raising the question whether exposure to social media polarise users or simply sort out like-minded voters based on their preexisting beliefs. Empirical research is in its infancy and the debate is still open.[10]

As Bob Brotherton emphasizes, "confirmation bias comes into play the moment we dwell on an idea".[11] This is not new: "The way we see things is a combination of what is there and of what we expected to find. The heavens are not the same to an astronomer as to a pair of lovers [...] Whatever we recognize as familiar we tend, if we are not very careful, to visualize with the aid of images already in our mind".[12]

Online information seekers seem thus being exposed to a *double filter*: a confirmation bias, on the one hand, and the algorithmic profiling of personal data, on the other. The proliferation of algorithms targets our interests and the attention prompted by our emotions.

As a consequence, the digital environment where users "freely choose" online contents (within a social network, a search engine or even a Telegram channel) is subject to a multifaceted constraint, affecting the nature

---

[10] Sloman and Fernbach (2017). See also Banks et al. (2020). For a critical review see Arguedas et al. (2022).

[11] Brotherton (2016).

[12] Lippmann (1922).

of the digital service, including, of course, platforms' economic gains from selling users' attention to advertisers.

Some of these facets refer to platforms' moderation policy, which equally, to a large extent, are performed by algorithms "scrutinising and moderating" contents with some human supervision. All the big platforms now provide a system of "whistleblowing" by users on illegal or harmful contents, according to their terms of service. However, the systems adopted and the timing of analysis and decision over whistleblowers' reports differ among platforms, as well as their pro-users policies. Moderation policies took the form of self-regulation, or commitments before public authorities (as in the case of Code of Conduct in Europe against disinformation and hate speech), but many of the outcomes and results still rely on whistleblowing and reporting, calling for a need of transparency and accountability.

These features raised in Europe the demand for a shift from self-regulation to co-regulation and to regulation of digital services, especially after the growth of online disinformation strategies in election periods and during the Covid-19 pandemic.

Indeed, disinformation and misinformation strategies in the web find a very fertile field of action in the environment created by platforms' algorithms as they enable them to reach precisely their online targets. Disinformation, as any advertised content, may successfully deploy algorithmic selection of contents to spread falsehoods with the aim of influencing political opinions or users' behaviour and attitudes towards distrust in democratic institutions. This explains why tackling online disinformation became on the main rationale for regulating platforms' digital services.

7.3   The Explosion of Online (Dis)Information

In March 2018, Sir Tim Berners-Lee, the creator of the web, wrote a long open letter for the 29th anniversary of the World Wide Web. The title was alarming: "*The web is under threat. Join us and fight for it*". In this letter, Berners-Lee asked how it was possible that what was once an open meta-platform, with a rich and vast selection of blogs and websites, became squashed under the weight of a few dominant platforms which devour their smaller rivals, and where a handful of companies can control how ideas and opinions are seen and shared and which "are able to lock in their position by creating barriers for competitors". According to Berners-Lee, "in recent years, we've seen conspiracy theories trend on social media platforms, fake Twitter and Facebook accounts stoke social tensions, external actors interfere in elections and criminals steal troves of personal data".

In this line, claims on influence and manipulation of election through organised online disinformation strategies by foreign groups have multiplied in many countries. Besides, the spread of hate speech on the web and social media, with the re-emergence of antisemitism and racism, has largely affected the online public sphere.

In May 2019, Antonio Guterres, UN Secretary General, outlined how "all over the world, we are witnessing a disturbing emergence of xenophobia, racism and intolerance, including growing anti-Semitism, anti-Muslimism hatred and persecution of Christians". Guterres' words still give us the sense of an emergency that has never subsided: "hatred is moving towards the mainstream, both in liberal democracies and in authoritarian systems". The year before, the European Commission against Racism and Intolerance (ECRI), established by the Council of Europe, denounced the increase in incitement to racial hatred and the phenomenon of xenophobic populism and their impact on the European political climate. In the 2018 report, later confirmed in 2019, the ECRI highlighted that "the growing fears of citizens regarding the economic situation and geopolitical and technological changes" had been exploited "by those who use migrants and minorities as scapegoats, and in particular by populist politicians who aim to divide societies on national, ethnic and religious lines". This practice, ECRI stressed, is followed "not only by political fringes, but has gained increasing space even in the more traditional parties and national governments, a phenomenon of great concern". Online hate speech is often sustained by the spread of falsehood or "misinformation" strategies.

On 4 March 2019, in his letter sent to the European citizens, the President of the French Republic, Emmanuel Macron, insisted there was a new threat across Europe: a "public speech that expresses hate or false information, that promises everything and is against everything".

Disinformation strategies are much more complex than simple fake news. They include an element of intentionality, repetitiveness, *systematicity* and *virality*, or *targeting* of the receiver regarding specific economic and/or political objectives. False information (yet susceptible to being received as true) is deliberately created to harm an individual, a social group, an organisation or a country, or to confirm/discredit and knowingly disseminate it for political, ideological or commercial purposes (including *click baiting*). They include: (a) *false context* (when true content is mixed with false information); (b) content influenced by false sources (content spread by false sources or false accounts impersonating authentic sources); (c) falsely created content (totally fake content, created to trick and /or harm); and (d) manipulated news (true information or images intentionally and deceptively manipulated).

A disinformation strategy is deliberately created to be believed by the receiver, who, via profiling of his/her data, reveals to the algorithm which issues could attract his/her attention. The algorithmic selection of online content, based on profiled data, provides to end users a personalised knowledge, i.e. precisely the type of (dis)information "demanded and needed" by users.

In the first months of 2017, CNN revealed the findings of a public inquiry into at least 100 websites specifically devoted to political information, all managed and owned by users originating from the city of Veles, a municipality in the Republic of Macedonia (a little more than 55,000 inhabitants), in which fake news was published in favour of Donald Trump. The inquiry highlighted that there was a specific strategy of disinformation, put in place by individual groups, aimed at earning revenues by selling online advertising from those websites. In September 2017, Facebook admitted that hundreds of fake accounts financed by the Internet Research Agency (IRA), a Russian company, had bought advertising space aimed at specific user categories before the presidential elections.

Over the last few years, disinformation strategies on social networks and various types of search engines for purposes of propaganda, manipulation, influence on electoral behaviours (including the 2020 US presidential elections) or on the information regarding the Covid19 pandemic and the risks associated to anti-Covid19 vaccines have exploded.

The explosion of disinformation that has involved various aspects of the Covid-19 virus fits into the cultural climate of distrust of science and conspiracy, outlined by Tim Bernes Lee. At the Monaco conference on security held in 2020, Tedros Adhanom Ghebreyesus, director general of World Health Organization, said: "we are not fighting a pandemic, we are fighting an' infodemic". Fake news, misinformation and conspiracy theories have become prevalent since the start of the COVID-19 pandemic.

According to Data Room,[13] 449 sites in the world spread false news about the new coronavirus, 274 are in the United States, 57 in France, 44 in Germany, 20 in the United Kingdom.

Faced with the explosion of disinformation on Covid-19, the European Commission has relaunched the "Code of good practices" adopted as a form of self-regulation by large online platforms, in agreement with the European Commission. The concern was that disinformation could undermine the trust of citizens in health institutions, encouraging phenomena of moral hazard and opportunism in the conduct of prevention of contagion.

The main online platforms reported on their updated policies and initiatives to reduce the spread of misinformation about COVID-19 vaccines in May 2021. For example, Facebook reported that COVID-19 vaccine "stickers" have been used by more than 5 million users in Worldwide. Additionally, more than 280 million people worldwide, including over 29 million people in the EU, visited the COVID-19 Information Centre created by Facebook during May 2021. During the month of May 2021 Facebook declared to have removed more than 62 thousand in the EU content on Facebook and Instagram, for breach of disinformation policies COVID-19 and vaccines. Google has introduced a feature available on Search, which presents users looking for information on COVID-19 vaccines, a list of authorised vaccines, statistics, and information about them. More information on where to get vaccinated is currently being implemented.

Finally, Twitter has updated notifications system when tweets are labelled or removed, based on "strike" that gradually make users more aware of their behaviours. These measures aimed at reducing the spread of disinformation about Covid-19 and related vaccines. Since the introduction of its COVID-19 guide Twitter declared to have challenged 11.7 million accounts, suspended 1,340 accounts and removed over 37,900 Tweets worldwide.

The explosion of online disinformation "is here to stay". It is not a temporary phenomenon due to users' behaviours, but the outcome of a complex objective dynamics and intended strategy in

---

[13] AGCOM (2018).

which economic targets (such as clickbaiting) and (geo)political strategies overlap, corrupting the online information system and threatening institutions and social cohesion.[14]

As more and more citizens, around the world, declare to get informed daily via social networks, disinformation strategies succeed at least in crafting the political *agenda setting* and the policy design in many crucial issues, such as climate change and health policies. In turn, this raises the fundamental question on the nature and evolution of online pluralism. Indeed, disinformation strategies may succeed as the online "public debate" turned to be highly fragmented, unverified, chaotic, self-selected and polarised.

7.4   Digital Services Design and the 'Pluralism Dilemma'

One of the reasons behind the success of on online disinformation strategies relies on what we can define the "platforms pluralism dilemma", i.e. the trade-off between the efficient matching between demand and supply provided by digital platforms, thanks to algorithmic profiling, and the pursuing of an open online pluralism.

Efficient "content" matching, indeed, generates the unintended consequence, especially for search engines and social networks, to virtually cancel from the user's informational sphere any content that is not "preferred" or that does not match with actual user's profiling. At the same time, "bad or false information" seem to go viral. Thus, on one side, online pluralism is reduced as more and more users tend to be less exposed to content and information that do not fit with their existing "preferences", and, on the other side, online discussion allows disinformation to get unchallenged.

The paradox here is that the spread of digital information through the web, and especially through social media, minimises the transaction costs for acquiring information compared to the mainstream traditional media. However, it also reduces the time spent searching for "relevant" and verified information. The decline of the traditional mainstream media has brought more freedom to get directly informed by alternative sources. However, and paradoxically, according to many scholars, this might lead

---

[14] Cosentino (2020).

to less pluralism and more polarisation. As Varian wrote in 1998, the Gresham Law, where *bad money drives out good*,[15] may well apply to information: "Low cost and low-quality information on the Internet can create problems for those who produce quality information".[16]

Over the last years, there have been many empirical studies conducted worldwide that have documented the driving force behind the selective attention of web users, focusing exclusively on the content which confirms their preconceived ideas, cancelling, forgetting, and underestimating everything that misrepresents those ideas. A recent report[17] empirically measured the importance of confirmation bias in the social media, as well as, its ability to create polarisation in ideas and public debate. According to the empirical analyses published in the report, information consumption models and user interaction with the news on the online platforms exhibit a strong tendency toward polarisation, selective exposure, homophily and the emergence of the so-called *echo chamber*. That is, according to these studies, users tended to select information consistent with their preferences and convictions, forming polarised groups of individuals with similar ideas on shared narratives and where conflicting information was ignored.

This leads us to the following question: are platforms' algorithms compatible with online pluralism? The first reaction is positive: the web allows more free speech and "free reach" than ever. However, algorithmic profiling may nonetheless induce a selection of contents that goes in an opposite direction to what is usually called pluralism. On the one side, the exposure to ideas and contents that not necessarily reflects our beliefs and preferences might be significantly reduced; on the other, the boost to falsehoods and disinformation might be exacerbated by matching "liars" and "phools". Polarised falsehoods may have, then, strong success in substituting diverse, plural and fact-based news. A phenomenon that may even alter, as Berners Lee claimed, electoral preferences (and results).

A recent study by Morpheus Cyber Security and APCO Worldwide has attempted to do a first analysis on the (inevitable) impacts on profiling distortions and, above all, on the *influence campaigns* on the Twitter platform during the 2018 midterm elections in Arizona and Florida. One

---

[15] Varian (1998).

[16] Sunstein (2017).

[17] AGCOM (2018).

of the findings is that, on average, a significant part of the support for candidates (27% in Arizona and 24% in Florida) came from *bots*, that is, from fake accounts or *robotics*. An example, which shows how at times the algorithm is guilty, becoming itself the object of opportunist behaviours resulting from the targeted disinformation campaigns which focus on making fake and polarised news viral, making *hashtags* popular with the assistance and orchestration of false accounts and robotics or foster specific contents in the Google and YouTube ranking to the detriment of others. In research published in 2017 by the Computational Propaganda Research Project of the Universities of Oxford, Woolley and Guibeault, the role of bots on Twitter were mapped during the 2016 US presidential campaigns, concluding in favour of the *measurable influence* that this type of propaganda has created.

Certain news is created or designed deliberately to target our emotions and become viral. The real truth loses its importance, or better, takes on the importance our emotions transfer to it. Apart from the eventual impact on voting results, it is easy to verify how *emotional disinformation* strategies influence, at least, *agenda setting*. These are extremely effective strategies as they gear the propaganda message depending on the receiver's characteristics, according to the so-called *resonance effect*.

Box 7.1 The Cambridge Analytica Case

A case that has dominated the news over the last years is the Cambridge Analytica scandal. Cambridge Analytica was a British company specialised in mining and processing an enormous amount of data from single individuals and user categories in order to create psychometric profiles useful for commercial and political micro-targeting strategies. Everything began with a Cambridge researcher, who had created a psychometric system, an app where each user could access Facebook with their own credentials. In granting their consent, the user allowed the app to harvest different information, even regarding their network of friends. According to the New York Times and Guardian estimates, from the initial number of 270,000 people, who had registered on the application using Facebook Login, this number would have reached, through friends of friends, the incredible number of 50 million Facebook profiles.

The problems began to emerge when Cambridge Analytica bought this data from the researcher, to then use it in political and electoral marketing. Millions of users were ready to receive personalised messages of emotional stimuli, electoral propaganda, and disinformation before going to the polls. Facebook was placed under investigation by the prosecutors of the Northern District of California regarding their dealings with Cambridge Analytica and, according to the *New York Times*, the Eastern District of New York conducted an investigation into the sharing of data with other companies (for commercial purposes) without prior consent or informing users.

In the United Kingdom, a report of the Digital, Culture, Media and Sport Committee, entitled Disinformation and "Fake News": Final Report, published on 18 February 2019, recreated the disinformation strategies adopted by the web and some social networks (such as Facebook) in the Brexit referendum and political elections, revealing evidence on foreign interference and reporting the websites, afterwards removed by Facebook, linked to these practices. The report concluded with a series of operative, legislative, and regulatory reform requests (which will be cited in the final chapter) concerning controls to be put in place on online platforms and social networks so as to prevent disinformation and digital dominance.

This issue cannot be seen as only one of privacy or transparency concerning the use of our data, as is often affirmed. The core point is how the algorithm may learn to provide a pluralistic outcome. Do users need new tools and rules to access everything, to reach everything, to discover the information they need, including information on the stream of news they receive and why—the so-called *discoverability rules.*

How can selective exposition, polarisation, disinformation be eliminated in order to produce diversity and expose us to the unexpected? As Sunstein[18] has suggested, we may need an algorithm to solve the problems of algorithm pluralism, balancing and mediating the content, defending it from strategies of disinformation and hate speech. This leads

---

[18] Sunstein (2019).

us back to the issue of digital services design in the online information system.

Some recent reforms in Europe have tried to tackle the issue of online pluralism. In Germany, in January 2018, the law NetzDG came into effect in order to force social network operators to remove any content clearly classifiable as hate speech within 24 hours of its being reported, while more contentious content can be withdrawn within seven days. Non-compliance with the law carries a fine of up to 50 million euros. In France, in November 2018, a law against fake news or online slander was approved. Election candidates, in the three months preceding voting, can appeal to the courts regarding any news they hold to be false or defamatory, obtaining its immediate withdrawal. Furthermore, the appeal can be lodged by a public body, a party or by any other subject claiming to be injured. The judge has 48 hours to establish if the news is fake or defamatory, and then order its withdrawal. The judge's ruling can be appealed against with a verdict to be pronounced within 48 hours. Offenders can be faced with imprisonment of up to one year and a fine of up to 75,000 euros. Moreover, there is the obligation of media that spreads offending news to reveal the identity of any financiers or advertisers.

These legislative approaches in Germany and France have been criticised due to the broad definitions of fake news and hate speech and the short time period to remove them. Instead, compared to the German case, under French law, the prevision to involve a third subject, the judge, to evaluate the case has been highly appreciated. In Italy, AGCOM, the Italian regulator for communications, has started a comparison of self-regulation procedure undertaken by search engines and social networks—in anticipation of the European Commission's approach for setting up the High-Level Group on Fake News and Online Disinformation. The focus of the Italian AGCOM and the European Commission concerned the online disinformation strategies regarding individual fake news, specifically looking at the links with the sources the strategies have originated from and the financing means, also through online advertising. Instead, in 2019, concerning hate speech, AGCOM approved a first regulation to counteract hate speech on radio and TV (the focus being, as for the British regulator OFCOM, how broadcasts are conducted and context accuracy), also foreseeing forms of co-regulation for online video-sharing platforms, in accordance with the lines set out in the Audio-visual Media Services Directive approved by the European Commission.

The problem, however, that arises is the inefficiency of a self-regulation when it is not thoroughly checked by independent authorities, equipped with inspection and auditing powers regarding data and algorithms, so as to verify the impact of the measures adopted.

Self-regulation has shown several limits. The relationship between the content, account, and advertising still needs to be investigated so as to hit offending or suspected subjects adopting disinformation and/or click baiting strategies.

In December 2018, the European Commission adopted an action plan to strengthen the cooperation between member states and the EU institutions in tackling the threats of disinformation, also involving the 2019 European elections. Facebook, Google, Twitter, and Mozilla voluntarily signed the code in October 2018, thereby being committed to:

a. block profits deriving from advertising by web profiles or websites that alter information, and provide advertisers with suitable security and information tools regarding websites that create disinformation;
b. allow the dissemination of political advertising messages to the public, and be committed to more ethical advertising;
c. have a clear and public policy on identity and online bots, and adopt measures to eliminate fake profiles;
d. provide information and tools to help individuals in making aware decisions and foster access to different perspectives involving issues of public interest, giving importance to authoritative sources;
e. provide searchers with an access to data complying with the principles of confidentiality, so they can follow and better understand the spread and repercussions of disinformation.

Facebook declared to have removed 364 pages in Russia originating from false identities, linked to Sputnik, a press agency in Moscow, signalling how some of these pages frequently spread anti-NATO news. Google declared to have removed, in only the month of January 2019, 6,226 advertising accounts in Italy and a total of 48,642 in the European Union which resulted in having violated the rules (false accounts, false identities, links with the spreading of fake news). As well, Facebook announced it had started up a collaboration with 25 independent fact-checking companies in 17 different languages (Italian included).

The Commission, though appreciating the commitment, has, however, declared to be extremely concerned about the unwillingness of the platforms to create specific indicators to measure the progress made, and the lack of detail in the results of the measures adopted on the capacity to adopt new policies and tools and adequate resources quickly. The underlying point remains the absence, up to now, of the possibility of third-party verification of the results presented and data flow inspections, also where its monetising is concerned. Therefore, at least the auditing and inspection powers of data economic use need to be handed over to independent and third-party subjects, such as authorities responsible for safeguarding pluralism. However, this needs to be done soon—the strategies of disinformation (and misinformation) are extremely fast and effective, with potential—as Berners-Lee recalled—deep and disruptive effects on free democratic debate and, at the end, on the functioning of our democracies.

Finally, in December 2020 the European Commission launched a proposal for a new regulation, called *Digital Services Act*, also to cope with disinformation issue as well as with transparency and accountability of self-regulation adopted by main digital platforms.

7.5 Towards a New Regulatory Design: The Digital Services Act

The Digital Service Act (DSA) expands and updates the key principles set out in the e-commerce directive, adopted in 2000 (which remains valid today) and sets the legal framework for the provision of digital services in the EU, by defining clear responsibilities and accountability for providers of intermediary services, according to their role, size and impact in the digital ecosystem. Moreover, the DSA proposal does not replace existing sectoral legislation, yet complement it, working as an *horizontal lex specialis*, cutting across all sectors in the economy, as far as digital services and online intermediaries are concerned. In particular, the DSA complements, among others, the Audiovisual Media Service Directive (AMSD), the Directive on Copyright in the Digital Single Market, and the horizontal Consumer Protection directives.[19] The legal basis of

---

[19] Audiovisual Media Service Directive: Directive (EU) 2018/1808. Directive on Copyright in the Digital Single Market: Directive (Eu) 2019/790. The main Directives on Consumer protection (Sect 4.3) are the Directive on unfair contract terms (Directive

this EU legislative proposal is Article 114 TFEU (internal market) and the legal form chosen is that of the Regulation (meaning there will be no need for Member States to take any implementing acts once the Regulation enters into force).

The main goals of the DSA are to (a) *contribute to the proper functioning of the internal market for [online] intermediary services* and (b) *set out uniform rules for a safe, predictable, and trusted online environment, where the fundamental rights enshrined in the Charter are effectively protected.*[20]

These objectives are pursued through the introduction of new rules on specific due diligence obligations for digital intermediaries and online platforms: i.e., responsibility for content, online user security, auditing, reporting, traceability, and transparency, as well as by establishing (i.e., confirming) a framework for their conditional exemption from liability.

The cornerstone indeed remains the principles enshrined in the e-commerce directive (Sect. 3.1). More specifically, the DSA proposal maintains: (a) an exemption from liability if providers of online intermediary services meet certain cumulative conditions set out in the DSA proposal[21]; (b) the prohibition—for the Member States—to impose on intermediation service providers a general monitoring or active obligation to seek facts or circumstances indicating illegal activity.

The European Commission also introduces the "good Samaritan" rule, borrowing and adapting that concept from the US legislation (Sect. 7.1), according to which intermediation service providers are not excluded from liability exemptions when they carry out voluntary activities to detect and remove content that is illegal or contrary to their "terms of services".

According to some, however, the goal of harmonising liability rules does not seem fully achieved[22]: the DSA only contains Union-wide rules

---

93/13/EC), the Directive of unfair commercial practices (Directiver 2005/29/EC), and the Consumer Rights Directive (Directive 2011/83/EC). All of them have been amended, in order to update the EU *consumer acquis* to the digitalisation, by the Directive on better enforcement and modernisation of EU consumer protection (Directive 2019/2161/EU).

[20] DSA Article 1.2.

[21] For example there isn't exemption from liability for those platforms that allow contracts between users and professionals in the event that the service makes it appear that the relevant product or information is provided by the online platform.

[22] Cauffman and Goanta (2021) and Buiten (2021).

on intermediary service providers' exemption from liability, nevertheless there is no Union-wide provisions on the conditions under which intermediary service providers incur liability. The conditions under which they incur liability are determined by other EU rules (not so clearly coordinated) or national law, thus limiting the capacity of the DSA to create a level playing field throughout the whole EU.[23]

The proposed DSA regulation sets out asymmetric obligations for online services, depending both on the nature of the services provided and the size of the providers (Table 7.1). In particular, DSA's obligations are differentiated, cumulative and are increasingly demanding for: (a) all intermediary services; (b) intermediaries providing hosting services; (c) online platforms; and (d) very large platforms. Those categories are built in such a way that each category includes all the following ones.

Referring to the wider category of services, the proposal identifies and defines, consistently with the e-commerce directive, intermediary services as mere conduit services (simple transmission), caching services (temporary storage in order to make transmission more efficient) or hosting (storage) services. Among them, hosting services are subject to additional obligations. Additional obligations are reserved for online platforms, and finally some more for very large online platforms. In this context, an online platform is defined as *"a provider of a hosting service which, at the request of a recipient of the service, stores and disseminates information to the public..."*,[24] which means that the information is made available to a potentially unlimited number of third parties; very large platforms are those having more than 45 million users or 10% of the EU population, thus posing greater risk in the dissemination of illegal contents and societal harms and consequently subject to additional specific rules and supervision.

---

[23] Cauffman and Goanta (2021) contest this approach of the EU Commission *"While the Explanatory Memorandum mentions that the liability exemptions as contained in the e-Commerce Directive received wide support from the stakeholders, it cannot be denied that this exemption has also been subject to criticism. For example, it has been argued that, in the case of online marketplaces, consumers often rely on the brand image of the platform and even consider the platform as their contracting party rather than the party who uses the platform to commercialise its goods and services.[...]All in all, the DSA appears to be more concerned with providing legal protection and certainty to intermediary service providers than to consumers using their services."*

[24] DSA Article 2 (h) (i).

Table 7.1 Obligation for online service in the DSA

	VERY LARGE PLATFORMS	ONLINE PLATFORMS	HOSTING SERVICES	ALL INTERMEDIARIES
Points of contact	●	●	●	●
Legal representatives	●	●	●	●
Terms and conditions	●	●	●	●
Reporting obligations	●	●	●	●
N&A	●	●	●	
Statement of reasons	●	●	●	
Complaint handling	●	●		
OOC	●	●		
Trusted flaggers	●	●		
Abusive behaviour	●	●		
KYBC	●	●		
Reporting criminal offences	●	●		
Advertising transparency	●	●		
Reporting obligations	●	●		
Risk assessment and mitigation	●			
Independent audits	●			
Recommender systems	●			
Enhanced advertising transparency	●			
Crisis protocols	●			
Data access and scrutiny	●			
Compliance officer	●			
Reporting obligations	●			

CUMULATIVE OBLIGATIONS!

Source EU Commission (2020)

Starting with the obligations applied to all intermediation services: general "due diligence" obligations, for example include the designation of a single point of contact, which communicates with the Authorities of the Member States, the Commission and the Committee pursuant to Article 47 of the regulation (appointing a legal representative in the EU if they are based outside the EU). Moreover, providers in their terms and conditions of service must clearly state any restrictions that will be imposed on users, and must be transparent about how and when illegal content, or content contrary to their terms and conditions, might be removed or disabled.

Online platforms are obliged to comply with additional obligations beyond the ones mentioned above: they must establish an internal complaints-handling system (easy to access and user-friendly); furthermore they have the obligation to engage with certified out-of-court dispute settlement bodies to resolve users' disputes. The proposed regulation also disciplines the role of *"trusted flaggers"*, i.e., entities that have demonstrated particular expertise and cooperation, in order to counter illegal content online: so online platform must give them priority in the handling of complaints, thus fast-tracking the procedure and increasing accuracy. Furthermore, the DSA enumerates measures against misuse of the online platform that must be adopted, such as temporarily suspending user accounts that frequently post manifestly illegal content. Facts and circumstances for making such determinations and the duration of the account suspension must be clearly delineated in the terms and conditions.

If, on the one hand, online platforms that qualify (pursuant to Recommendation 2003/361/EC) as micro or small enterprises are excluded from the additional obligations, on the other hand very large online platforms are instead obliged to comply with additional rules to mitigate the systemic risk[25] stemming from the dissemination of illegal content through their services: from any negative effects for the exercise of certain fundamental rights (respect for private and family life, freedom of expression and information) to the intentional manipulation of their service. In particular, at least once a year, those platforms have to conduct systemic risk assessments deriving from the operation and use of their services in

---

[25] The additional transparency and due diligence obligations on online platforms and very large online platforms recognise the key role they can play in curbing illegal and problematic content. Buiten (2021).

the EU and take reasonable and effective measures to mitigate these risks. Moreover, very large platforms have to appoint a compliance officer and must be evaluated by external and independent parties that verify the compliance with the regulation.[26] The relevant point of the proposal here, with respect to the use of self-learning algorithms, concerns the obligation of transparency in relation to the main parameters of the decision-making algorithms used to offer content on platforms (the ranking mechanism) and the options provided to the user to modify these parameters: the platforms are required to offer users at least one option that is not based on profiling.

Regulation, in its current formulation, also establishes the obligation for those very large platforms to provide the Digital Service Coordinator (which each member state has to identify as the main enforcer) or the Commission itself with access to the data necessary to monitor their compliance with the DSA. Such data, with the limits and modalities envisaged, must be released to academic researchers who carry out research on systemic risks. The DSA also contains specific requirements for enhanced supervision of large online platforms in case they violate the above obligations. Furthermore, the European Commission is empowered to intervene if the infringement persists.

The theme that is most intertwined with the role of algorithms and artificial intelligence refers to the introduction of the obligations that hosting services and online platforms of all size must fulfil as regards the removal of alleged "illegal content". One of the central aspects of the DSA, aimed to counteract the spread of illicit content, is in fact related to the content moderation policies, implemented by algorithms and therefore by artificial intelligence mechanisms based on self-learning processes.

However, it should be emphasised that the DSA does not harmonise the definition of illegal content (product or service), it just harmonises procedures. The definition of illegal content depends on what is to be considered illegal under other piece of legislation at European or national level. Commission's decision not to propose direct regulation of illegal content is not surprising, because of the difficult trade-offs involved. For

---

[26] For C. Cauffman and Goanta (2021) these measures are an example of outsourcing regulatory powers to private parties "*The identification and solution of risks is thus in the first instance left to the very large online platforms themselves, and compliance with their specific obligations is outsourced to private audit firms*".

some time now, member states' policy makers have been faced with the difficulty, on the one hand, of defining the case in more detail, and, on the other hand, of not restricting freedom of expression. This concern is also evident in the DSA by the number of obligations that provide redress mechanisms to users experiencing content removals and account suspensions.

The main policy points here are two: (i) defining "illegal content" and (ii) having access to the algorithmic methods of identifying such contents. The definition of illegal content contains a twofold aspect, on one side, contents explicitly prohibited by current legislation, such as child pornography, cyberbullying and so on; on the other side, content not complying with the principles, rules and codes of conduct set by platforms's rule (terms of service), i.e., considered harmful yet not per se necessary illegal, such as hate speech, disinformation, and so on. Generally speaking, there is a differentiated treatment between illegal information (e.g., hate speech, incitement to violence or defamatory statements) and harmful non-illegal content, which the DSA does not impose to be removed. The main novelty consists in the right of third parties to be able to access an easy-to-use online procedure, through which it is possible to notify the supplier of alleged illegal content. On the other side, if the intermediary removes that content, the user whose content has been removed or disabled has the right, however, to be promptly provided with the reasons why the decision was made, as well as with the possibility to contest the intermediary's decision, including when the decision is based on platform's terms and conditions. In particular, users can can compliant directly with the platform, choose an out-of-court dispute settlement body or seek redress before courts.[27]

Jurisdiction over an online intermediary will depend on the intermediary's main place of establishment or, in the case of intermediaries not established in a Member State (yet in scope of DSA application when

---

[27] On this point C. Cauffman and Goanta (2021) affirms that "It is true that recipients remain free to apply for redress before the competent courts. However, it is likely that for many non-professional recipients the costs of judicial procedures will function as a disincentive. Dispute resolution is therefore likely to remain mainly in the hands of private actors. While it is understandable that an internal dispute resolution system is required, the question arises as to whether, particularly in cases where free speech is at stake, the facilitation of access to court proceedings through the introduction of harmonised rules limiting the costs of such proceedings would not be more suitable than the promotion of out-of-court dispute settlement".

offering services within the EU), on the position of the designated EU legal representative.

However, since providers, and in particular large platforms, often operate at least on a pan-European basis and, more often, globally, the article 47 of DSA also sets up an advisory group composed of the Digital Services Coordinators of each Member State, called the "European Board for Digital Services"(the committee). The Committee will be in charge of assisting individual coordinators of digital services and the Commission in the supervision of very large online platforms, as well as coordinating activities for the enforcement of the regulation (including joint investigations), where necessary, and will supervise the activities of the coordinators of digital services.

Considering those rules on how platforms, notably large ones, moderate content, the DSA, jointly with the European Democracy Action Plan (EDAP),[28] represent a step change for the EU policy on disinformation—clearly moving from self-regulation to co-regulation. The European Democracy Action Plan sets out measures around three main pillars: (i) promotion of free and fair elections; (ii) strengthening media freedom and pluralism; and (iii) counter disinformation. While the DSA proposal, as an horizontal act, works mostly indirectly against the spread of disinformation, by tackling 'manipulation' aimed to amplify harmful behaviours, mainly via the mitigation of the systemic risk that large platforms may create. The DSA regulation, proposed by the EU Commission, is currently under political approval by the EU Parliament and the EU Council. It is therefore subject to further evolution and adjustments. In any event, the DSA is an effective regulation of digital services that, despite some limitations and omissions, seems to be heading in the direction requested by users' associations and needed by EU citizens, who are exposed to ever-increasing risks, such as the spread of illegal and harmful content and unsafe products as well as biased access to information, and some forms of limitations to conscious choice or free expression.

As repeatedly highlighted throughout the entire book, digital intermediaries and online platforms have become integral parts of our daily lives, economies, and societies. Today, our activities, our identities, and most our entire selves are (also) expressed and developed within what

---

[28] European Commission (2020b).

we have called the 'digital market society'. Consequently, a clear definition of fundamental digital rights is essential to tackle those risks that can have a far-reaching effect for citizens, companies, the principles of fair and efficient markets, and the fundaments of democratic values. Indeed, the digital transformation does not justify exceptions to the rights and freedoms that the EU citizens and companies enjoy under EU law, according to the EU mantra "*what is illegal offline must be illegal online*". However, it is important to underline that the digital market society, along with its rights and freedoms, is not independent from offline markets and society. The ultimate digital policy goal should be to shape such a digital ecosystem able to provide people with a better quality of life, in the real life, as well as to support the fulfilment of their core values and needs, not selected through algorithms, yet shaped by history, traditions, vis à vis conversation, and non-intermediated feelings. Of course, a satisfactory level of online rights' protection is a fundamental crucial step, but it is just an intermediate goal. Or better, it is a means to reinforce and enhance overall rights and freedom and fully exploit new opportunities for individuals and companies, as well as a sustainable economic growth and innovation dynamic. This is the profound sense of a human-centred digital transformation: to evaluate, steer, and shape the digital world in the light of its impact on people's life. And this is what the DSA-DMA package aims to do, as well as the GDPR and the Data Act, the Consumer protection modernisation, and the wider EU digital policies (i.e., the deployment of secure and high-performing digital infrastructures; facilitation of digital transition of businesses; development of people's digital skills and literacy; and digitalisation of essential public services). This is also the explicit objective of the 2022 *Declaration on digital rights and principles* (Sect. 4.1) which builds on the EU Treaties, the EU Charter of fundamental rights, and the case-law of the EU Court of Justice. As sometimes underlined in the book, some of the above-mentioned acts and policies should be coordinated in a more systemic way, and some aspects could be improved or better defined. Perhaps, some of them would prove to be not completely effective and will require adjustments or revisions. Nevertheless, it is common belief that the EU digital policy's overarching direction and overall approach is the right one and the predominant evaluation is very positive. Conceiving, building, and enforcing an effective, efficient, and fair regulation of digital markets and societies is indeed a very complex and long journey. The European Union is still approaching such a challenging but indispensable destination, by building a *Digital compass* that is progressively tracing 'paths' towards the *Digital future of Europe* (and of the whole world). While we still find ourselves in this journey, all shall keep in mind what Tolkien told us in 1954 and is still true today, in the 'digital-earth': *"not all those who wander are lost"*.

REFERENCES

AGCOM. (2018). *News vs. fake in the information system.* Interim Report of sector inquiry "online platforms and the information system".

Arguedas, A. R., Robertson, C., Fletcher, R., & Nielsem, R. (2022). *Echo chambers, filter bubbles, and polarisation: A literature review.* Report of the Reuters Institute.

Banks, A., Calvo, E., Karol, D., & Telhami, S. (2020). #PolarizedFeeds: Three experiments on polarization, framing, and social media. *International Journal of Press/Politics, 26*(3), 609–634.

Brotherton, R. (2016). *Suspicious minds: Why we believe conspiracy theories.* Bloomsbury Sigma.

Buiten Miriam C. B. (2021) *The Digital Services Act: From intermediary liability to platform regulation.* Working Paper.

Cauffman, C., & Goanta, C. (2021). A new order: The Digital Services Act and consumer protection. *European Journal of Risk Regulation,* 1–17. https://doi.org/10.1017/err.2021.8

Cosentino, G. (2020). *Social media and the post-truth world order.* Palgrave Macmillan.

Epstein, R., & Robertson, R. (2015). Search engine manipulation effect (SEME). *Proceedings of the National Academy of Sciences, 112*(33), 4512–4521.

European Commission. (2020a). Proposal for a Regulation on a single market for digital services (digital services act, DSA) and amending directive 2000/31/EC (e-commerce Directive).

European Commission. (2020b). Communication on European democracy action plan. COM/2020/790 final.

Lippmann, W. (1922). *Essay on public opinion.*

Persson, P. (2018). Attention manipulation and information overload. *Behavioural Public Policy, 2*(1), 78–106.

Simon, H. (1971). Design organizations for an information-rich world. In M. Greenberg (Ed.), *Computer communication and the public interest* (pp. 37–52). Johns Hopkins University Press.

Sloman, S., & Fernbach, P. (2017). *The knowledge illusion.* Riverhead Books.

Sunstein, C. (2001). *Republic.com.* Princeton University Press.

Sunstein, C. (2017). *#republic: Divided democracy in the age of social media.* Princeton University Press.

Sunstein, C. (2019). Algorithms, correcting biases. *Social Research: An International Quarterly, 86*(2), 499–511.

Sunstein, C. (2020). *Too much information.* MIT Press.

Sunstein, C. (2021). *Liars. Falsehoods and free speech in an age of deception.* Oxford University Press.

Tolkien, J. R. R. (1954). *The fellowship of the ring.*

Varian, H. (1998). *Markets for information goods.*

9 783030 893873